CASSEROLES

Margaret Fulton's
BOOK OF
CASSEROLES

OCTOPUS

CONTENTS

Fish & Shellfish	6
Beef	20
Veal	30
Lamb	36
Pork	46
Poultry & Game	54
Vegetables	70
Pulses, Rice, Pasta & Cheese	80
Index	94

This edition published 1989
by Octopus Illustrated Publishing
Michelin House, 81 Fulham Road
London SW3 6RB
part of Reed International Books

Reprinted 1991, 1992

Copyright © Reed International Books Limited 1979

ISBN 0 7064 5017 5

Produced by Mandarin Offset
Printed and bound in Hong Kong

INTRODUCTION

A robust casserole on the table is a comforting sight indeed. The rich flavour of slow-cooked food, with its own flavoursome juices and the heady smell when the lid is taken off is one of the rewards of winter, which seems to be the ideal time for a casserole.

Not all casseroles take hours to cook, some may be put together from leftovers or convenience foods and can be ready in half-an-hour. Casseroles may be made from all kinds of ingredients such as fish, meat, poultry, vegetables, pulses, rice and cheese.

Casserole cookery is usually economical and easy, important if you are a working woman who has a family to feed or likes to entertain, for most casseroles actually taste better for having been made a day or two before required.

Whether you are feeding a hungry family or giving a dinner party you will find casseroles suitable for every occasion in this exciting new cookbook.

Margaret Fulton

NOTES

Standard spoon and cup measurements are used in all recipes
1 teaspoon = one 5 ml spoon
1 tablespoon = one 20 ml spoon
All spoon measures are level.
1 cup = 250 ml

Fresh herbs are used unless otherwise stated. If unobtainable substitute a bouquet garni of the equivalent dried herbs, or use dried herbs instead but halve the quantities stated.

Freshly ground black pepper should be used unless white pepper is specified.

Ovens should be preheated to the specified temperature.

For all recipes, quantities are given in both metric and imperial measures. Follow either set of measures but not a mixture of both, because they are not interchangeable.

FISH & SHELLFISH

Whole Fish with Tomato Sauce

3 x 500 g (1 lb) whole fish (snapper, mullet, bream, etc.), cleaned
2 tablespoons plain flour
salt and pepper
75 g (2½ oz) butter
1 onion, chopped
1 green pepper, cored, seeded and chopped
1 red pepper, cored, seeded and chopped
2 celery sticks, chopped
2 x 400 g cans tomatoes
1 tablespoon tomato paste
1 tablespoon Worcestershire sauce
1 tablespoon lemon juice
few drops of Tabasco sauce
1 bay leaf
parsley sprigs to garnish

Rinse the fish and pat dry with kitchen paper. Season the flour and rub this all over the fish, inside and out. Place the fish in a casserole or baking dish into which it fits snugly.

Melt the butter in a saucepan. Add the onion, green and red peppers and celery and fry until the onion is softened. Stir in the tomatoes with their juice, tomato paste, Worcestershire sauce, lemon juice, Tabasco and the bay leaf. Bring to the boil and simmer for 15 minutes or until the vegetables are tender.

Remove the bay leaf, then purée the sauce by rubbing through a sieve or working in an electric blender. Adjust the seasoning, then pour the sauce around the fish. Cook in a preheated moderate oven, 180°C (350°F), for 25 minutes or until the fish is tender. Baste the fish frequently with the sauce during cooking. Garnish with parsley.

Serves 4 to 6

Prawns in Herb Butter

1 kg (2 lb) unshelled raw prawns
salt and pepper
7 cups water
125 g (4 oz) butter
2 tablespoons chopped parsley
3 tablespoons chopped fresh herbs as available (preferably tarragon and basil)
juice of ½ lemon
chopped parsley to garnish

Cook the prawns in lightly salted boiling water for about 5 minutes or until pink. Drain and allow to cool slightly, then remove the shells.

Cream together the butter, parsley, herbs, salt and pepper to taste and the lemon juice. Spread half the herb butter over the bottom of a flameproof baking dish. Press the prawns into the butter, in rows, and cover with the remaining herb butter.

Cook in a preheated moderately hot oven, 200°C (400°F), for 10 minutes. Pop the dish under a preheated grill and cook for a few more minutes or until the top browns. Garnish with parsley.

Serves 4

NOTE: If raw prawns are unobtainable, substitute 500 g (1 lb) frozen, shelled prawns. Do not precook; simply thaw before adding to the herb butter.

Whole fish with tomato sauce; Prawns in herb butter; Mediterranean fish steaks (page 8).

Mediterranean Fish Steaks

4 tablespoons olive oil
2 onions, thinly sliced
1 clove garlic, finely chopped
1 green pepper, cored, seeded and sliced in rings
4 large tomatoes, skinned and sliced
2 teaspoons dried basil
salt and pepper
4 white fish steaks
2 teaspoons lemon juice
6 tablespoons dry white wine

Heat the oil in a frying pan and fry the onions and garlic until softened. Add the green pepper rings and continue frying for 3 minutes. Remove from the heat and place half the mixture in a casserole.

Arrange half the tomato slices on top and sprinkle with half the basil and salt and pepper to taste. Place the fish steaks on top and sprinkle with the lemon juice. Add the rest of the tomato slices, basil and onion and green pepper mixture. Pour in the wine.

Cover and cook in a preheated moderate oven, 180°C (350°F), for about 45 minutes or until the fish is tender.
Serves 4

Illustrated on page 7.

Casseroled Shellfish

750 g (1½ lb) potatoes
salt and pepper
45 g (1½ oz) butter
2 tablespoons plain flour
¾ cup milk
¾ cup dry white wine
250 g (8 oz) canned crabmeat, drained and flaked
375 g (12 oz) frozen shelled prawns, thawed
1 small onion, grated
3 tablespoons chopped parsley
¾ cup grated Cheddar cheese
watercress sprigs to garnish

Parcook the potatoes in boiling salted water for 10 minutes, then drain and slice thinly.

Melt 30 g (1 oz) of the butter in a saucepan. Add the flour and cook, stirring, for 1 minute. Gradually stir in the milk and wine and bring to the boil. Simmer, stirring, until thickened. Add salt and pepper to taste and fold in the crabmeat, prawns, onion, parsley and cheese.

Layer one third of the potato slices in a greased casserole. Cover with half the fish mixture. Repeat the layers, finishing with a layer of potato slices. Dot with the remaining butter.

Cook in a preheated moderate oven, 180°C (350°F), for about 45 minutes or until the potatoes are tender and the top is crisp. Garnish with watercress.
Serves 4

Greek Prawn Casserole

1¼ cups water
juice of ½ lemon
1 kg (2 lb) unshelled raw prawns
3 tablespoons olive oil
1 onion, finely chopped
1 clove garlic, crushed
2 x 400 g cans tomatoes, drained and chopped
¾ teaspoon dried oregano
salt and pepper
90 g (3 oz) Fetta cheese, crumbled

Bring the water and lemon juice to the boil in a saucepan. Add the prawns and simmer for 5 minutes or until pink. Drain, reserving the liquid, cool slightly, then remove the shells. Boil the liquid until reduced to ⅔ cup.

Heat the oil in a flameproof casserole. Add the onion and garlic and fry until softened. Stir in the tomatoes, oregano, reserved prawn cooking liquid and salt and pepper to taste. Simmer until the sauce is reduced and thickened.

Fold the prawns into the sauce. Sprinkle the cheese on top and cook in a preheated moderate oven, 180°C (350°F), for 15 minutes.

Serves 4

NOTE: If raw prawns are unobtainable, substitute 500 g (1 lb) frozen, shelled prawns. Do not precook; simply thaw and add them to the cooked sauce. For the cooking liquor use ⅔ cup water and 2 teaspoons lemon juice.

Fish Mornay

500 g (1 lb) spinach
salt and pepper
60 g (2 oz) butter
125 g (4 oz)
  mushrooms, sliced
750 g-1 kg (1½-2 lb)
  fish fillets, skinned
⅓ cup plain flour
2 cups milk
grated nutmeg
⅓ cup grated
  Gruyère cheese
½ cup grated
  Cheddar cheese
parsley sprigs to
  garnish

Cook the spinach, with only the water clinging to the leaves after washing, until tender. Drain well, pressing out all excess water, then chop. Season with salt and pepper to taste and stir in 15 g (½ oz) of the butter. Spread the spinach over the bottom of a greased casserole. Cover with the mushrooms and arrange the fish fillets on top.

Melt the remaining butter in a saucepan. Add the flour and cook, stirring, for 1 minute. Gradually stir in the milk and bring to the boil. Simmer, stirring, until thickened. Season to taste with salt, pepper and nutmeg, then stir in all but 2 tablespoons of the cheese.

Pour the cheese sauce over the fish and sprinkle the reserved cheese on top. Cook in a preheated moderate oven, 180°C (350°F), for about 30 minutes or until the fish is tender. Garnish with parsley.
Serves 4

Herby Fish Casserole

500 g (1 lb) fish fillets
15 g (½ oz) butter
1 tablespoon plain flour
1 cup milk
¼ teaspoon garlic salt
¼ teaspoon dried thyme
¼ teaspoon dried oregano
6 spring onions, finely chopped
salt and pepper
paprika

Arrange the fish fillets in a greased baking dish. Melt the butter in a saucepan. Add the flour and cook, stirring, for 1 minute. Gradually stir in the milk and bring to the boil. Simmer, stirring, until thickened. Stir in the garlic salt, herbs, spring onions and salt and pepper to taste. Pour over the fish and sprinkle with a little paprika.

Cook in a preheated moderate oven, 180°C (350°F), for 30 minutes or until the fish is tender.
Serves 4

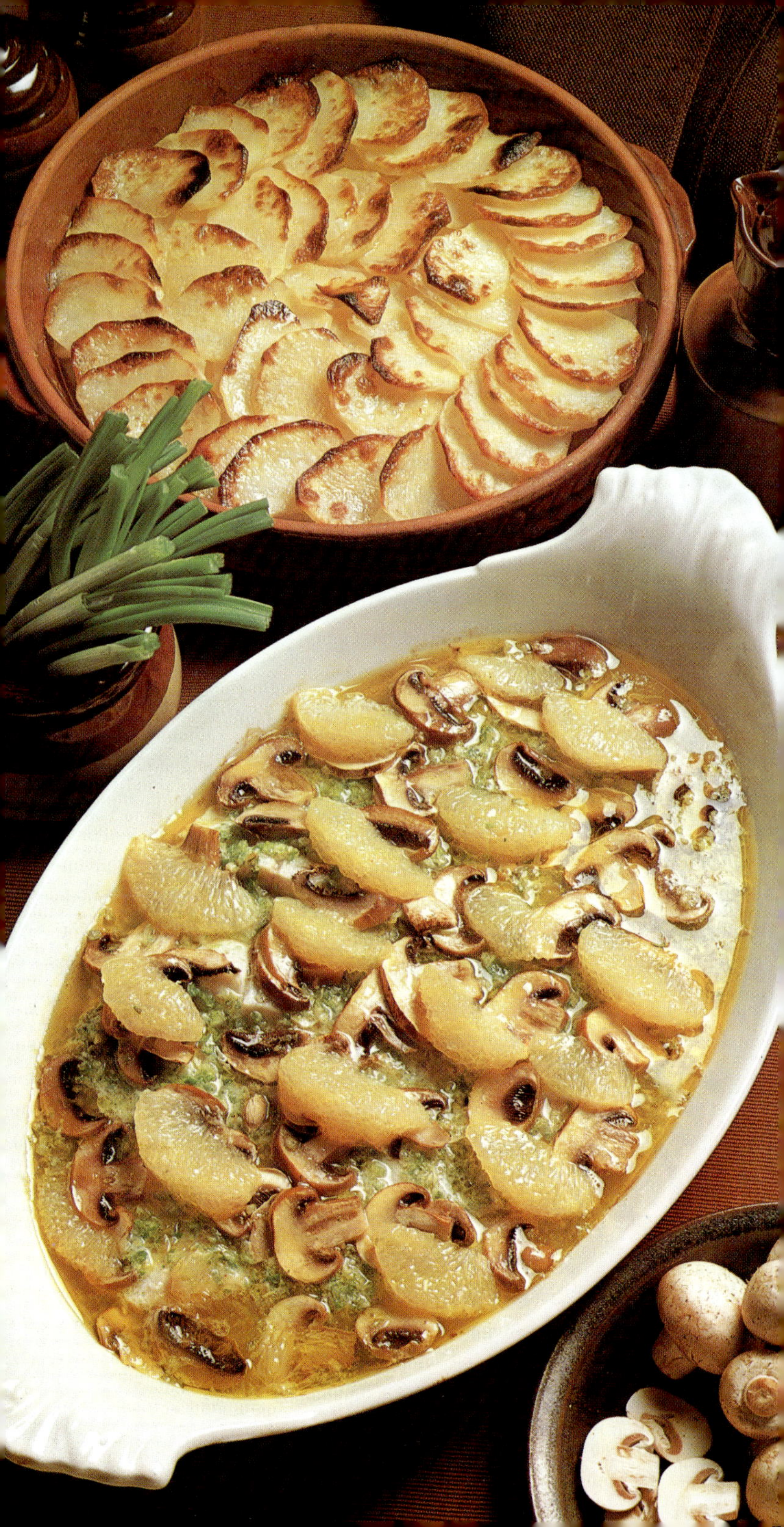

Fish Boulangère

500 g (1 lb) potatoes
salt and pepper
60 g (2 oz) butter
1 clove garlic, very finely chopped
750 g (1½ lb) white fish fillets, skinned and cut into chunks
1 large onion, thinly sliced

Parcook the potatoes in boiling salted water for 10 minutes. Drain and slice thinly.

Cream half the butter with the garlic and spread over the bottom of a casserole. Arrange the fish chunks on top and sprinkle with salt and pepper. Cover with the onion and then the potato slices. Dot with the remaining butter.

Cook in a preheated moderate oven, 180°C (350°F), for about 40 minutes or until the fish and potatoes are tender.
Serves 4

Bream with Grapefruit and Mushrooms

4 bream fillets, skinned
60 g (2 oz) butter
3 spring onions, chopped
salt and pepper
2 grapefruit
125 g (4 oz) mushrooms, sliced

Arrange the bream fillets in a greased casserole. Mash the butter with the spring onions and salt and pepper to taste. Grate the rind from the grapefruit and beat into the butter. Spread this over the fish fillets. Cover with the mushrooms.

Squeeze the juice from one grapefruit and peel and segment the other. Pour the grapefruit juice over the mushrooms and place the grapefruit segments on top.

Cover and cook in a preheated moderate oven, 180°C (350°F), for about 30 minutes or until the fish is cooked.
Serves 4

Smoked Fish au Gratin

500 g (1 lb) smoked fish fillets
milk for poaching
60 g (2 oz) butter
¼ cup plain flour
¾ cup cream
salt and pepper
½ cup grated Cheddar cheese
½ cup fresh breadcrumbs
parsley sprigs to garnish

Put the fish fillets in a saucepan, pour over enough milk to cover and poach gently for 15 minutes. Drain, reserving the milk, and flake the fish.

Melt the butter in a clean saucepan. Add the flour and cook, stirring, for 2 minutes. Gradually stir in the cream and ¾ cup of the reserved poaching milk. Bring to the boil, stirring, and simmer until thickened. Season with salt and pepper to taste. Stir in all but 1 tablespoon of the cheese and when it has melted fold in the flaked fish. Turn into a greased casserole.

Mix together the breadcrumbs and remaining cheese and sprinkle over the top. Cook in a preheated moderatly hot oven, 190°C (375°F), for 20 minutes or until the top is golden brown. Garnish with parsley.
Serves 4

Fish with Horseradish Cream

1 kg (2 lb) white fish cutlets
1¼ cups fish or chicken stock
1 tablespoon lemon juice
45 g (1½ oz) butter
⅓ cup plain flour
⅔ cup cream
1 tablespoon horseradish sauce
salt and pepper
chopped chives to garnish

Arrange the fish in one layer in a baking dish. Pour over the stock and lemon juice and cook in a preheated moderately hot oven, 200°C (400°F), for 15 to 20 minutes or until almost cooked.

Drain off the cooking liquid into a saucepan; keep the fish warm. Boil the liquid until it is reduced to ⅔ cup.

Melt the butter in a clean saucepan. Add the flour and cook, stirring, for 2 minutes. Gradually stir in the reduced cooking liquid and bring to the boil, stirring. Stir in the cream, horseradish sauce and salt and pepper to taste. Pour this sauce over the fish and return to the oven. Cook for a further 15 minutes. Serve garnished with chives.

Serves 4

Salt Cod and Celery Bake

500 g (1 lb) dried salt cod, soaked overnight
45 g (1½ oz) butter
⅓ cup plain flour
2 cups milk (or half fish stock and half milk)
pinch of dry mustard
salt and pepper
1 egg, beaten
2 cups fresh breadcrumbs
4 celery sticks, finely chopped
tomato slices to garnish

Drain the cod and place in a saucepan. Cover with fresh water and bring to the boil. Simmer for 20 minutes, then drain well. Skin, bone and flake the fish.

Melt the butter in another saucepan. Add the flour and cook, stirring, for 2 minutes. Gradually stir in the milk (or stock and milk) and bring to the boil. Simmer, stirring, until thickened. Add the mustard and salt and pepper to taste. Remove from the heat and cool slightly, then beat in the egg.

Place half the cod in a greased baking dish. Cover with half the breadcrumbs, half the celery, then half the sauce. Repeat the layers.

Cook in a preheated moderately hot oven, 190°C (375°F), for 20 minutes. Garnish with tomato slices.

Serves 4

Tuna Noodle Casserole

500 g (1 lb) noodles
salt and pepper
1 x 300 g can condensed cream of mushroom soup
2 tablespoons medium sherry
2 x 185 g cans tuna fish, drained and flaked
6 spring onions, finely chopped
4 hard-boiled eggs, sliced
30 g (1 oz) potato crisps, crushed
2 tablespoons grated Parmesan cheese
parsley sprigs to garnish

Cook the noodles in boiling salted water until tender. Drain well, then mix in the soup and sherry. Put about one third of the noodle mixture in a greased casserole. Cover with half the tuna, spring onions and eggs, then season with salt and pepper to taste. Repeat the layers and top with the remaining noodle mixture.

Mix together the crisps and cheese and sprinkle over the top. Cook in a preheated moderate oven, 180°C (350°F), for 25 to 30 minutes or until the top is golden brown. Garnish with parsley.

Serves 4 to 6

Gemfish in Cider

750 g (1½ lb) gemfish fillets, skinned and cut into chunks
2 eating apples, cored and sliced
2 celery sticks, chopped
1 teaspoon chopped sage
salt and pepper
1¼ cups dry cider
15 g (½ oz) butter
1 tablespoon plain flour

Put the fish in a greased flameproof casserole and cover with the apple slices and celery. Sprinkle with the sage and salt and pepper to taste, then pour in the cider.

Cover and cook in a preheated moderate oven, 180°C (350°F), for 25 to 35 minutes or until the fish is tender.

Transfer the fish and apple slices to a warmed serving dish and keep hot.

Blend the butter with the flour to make a smooth paste. Add a little of the hot cooking liquid, then stir this into the remaining liquid in the casserole. Bring to the boil on top of the stove, stirring, and simmer until thickened, then pour over the fish.

Serves 4

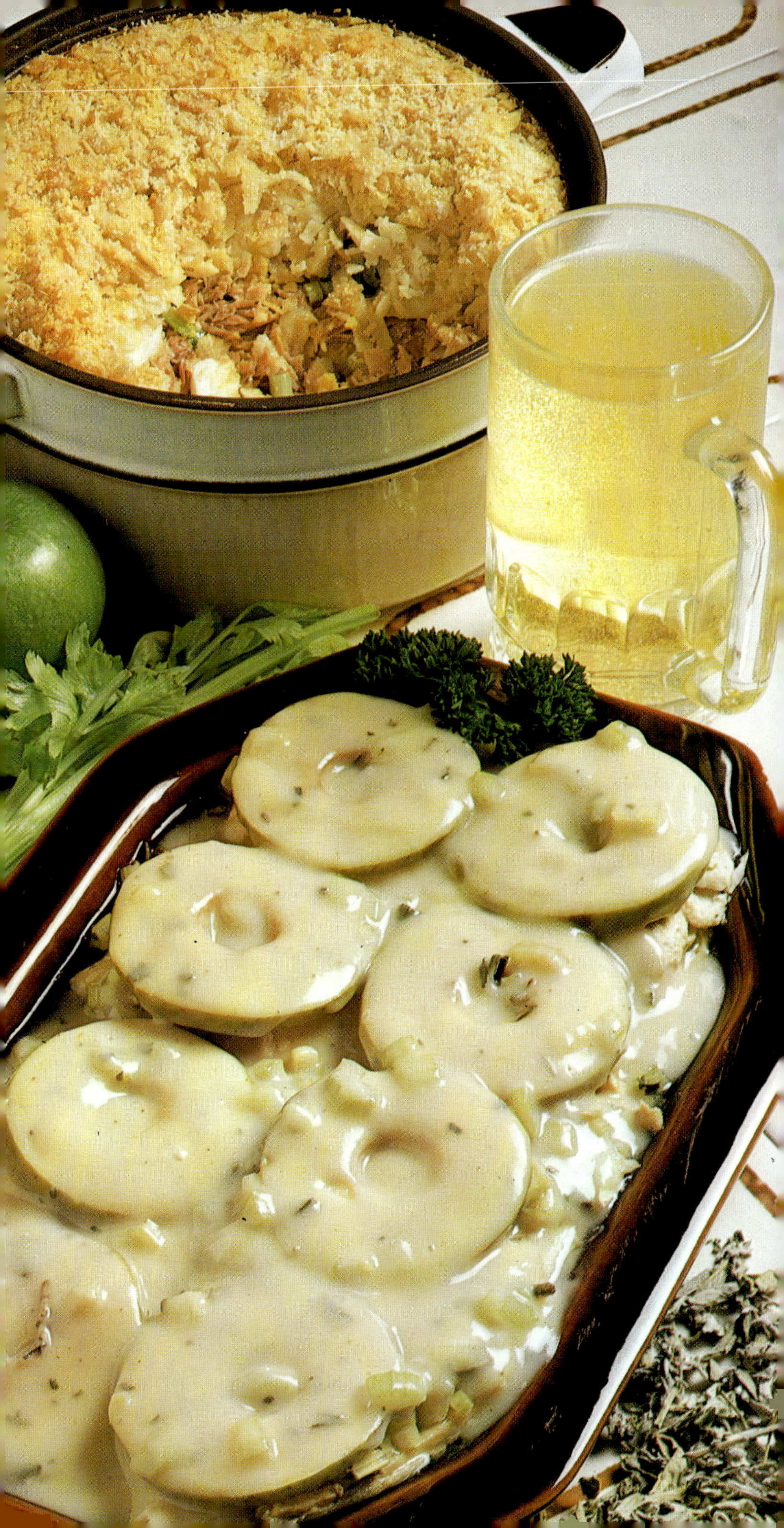

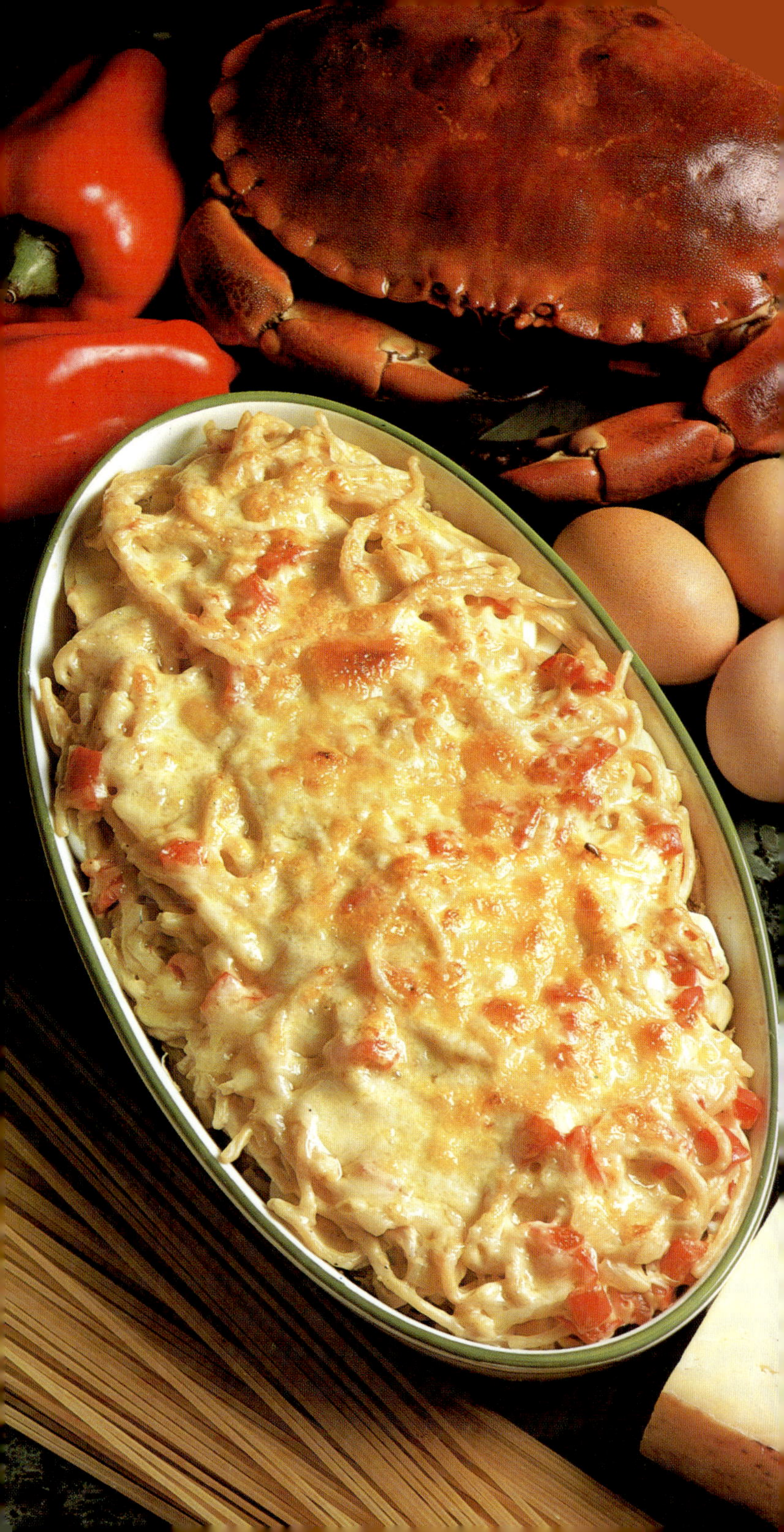

Crab and Spaghetti Bake

185 g (6 oz) spaghetti
salt and pepper
30 g (1 oz) butter
1 large onion, chopped
1 medium red pepper, cored, seeded and diced
¼ cup plain flour
1¼ cups milk
⅔ cup cream
2 teaspoons French mustard
1 tablespoon Worcestershire sauce
250 g (8 oz) cooked fresh, or canned crabmeat, drained and flaked
4 hard-boiled eggs, sliced
1 cup grated mature Cheddar cheese

Break the spaghetti into short lengths and cook in boiling salted water until just tender. Meanwhile, melt the butter in a saucepan, add the onion and red pepper and sauté until softened. Stir in the flour and cook, stirring, for 1 minute, then gradually stir in the milk and cream. Bring to the boil and simmer, stirring, until thickened. Stir in the mustard, Worcestershire sauce and salt and pepper to taste.

Drain the spaghetti and fold into the sauce. Spread half this mixture in a greased shallow casserole. Cover with the crabmeat, then the sliced eggs and top with the remaining spaghetti sauce. Sprinkle the cheese over the top. Cook in a preheated moderately hot oven, 190°C (375°F), for 25 minutes or until heated through and bubbling.

Serves 4 to 6

BEEF

Italian Pot Roast

1-1.25 kg (2-2½ lb) piece of beef topside
salt and pepper
3 tablespoons olive oil
1 onion, chopped
1 clove garlic, crushed
2 large carrots, sliced
2 celery sticks, sliced
1 x 215 g can tomatoes, drained and chopped
1¼ cups dry red wine
1 teaspoon dried oregano
1 bay leaf

Rub the beef all over with salt and pepper. Heat the oil in a flameproof casserole, add the beef and brown on all sides, then remove from the casserole.

Add the onion, garlic, carrots and celery to the casserole and fry until the onion is softened. Stir in the tomatoes, wine, oregano and bay leaf and bring to the boil.

Return the beef to the casserole and turn over in the liquid. Cover tightly and cook in a preheated moderate oven, 180°C (350°F), for 3 hours or until the meat is tender. Baste occasionally during the cooking.

Remove the beef from the casserole, place on a warmed serving plate and keep hot.

Boil the cooking liquid on top of the stove until well reduced and thickened. Strain and serve as a sauce, with the beef.

Serves 4

Italian Beef Casserole

2 tablespoons olive oil
1 onion, chopped
1 clove garlic, crushed
4 bacon rashers, derinded and diced
2 carrots, diced
1 celery stick, diced
500 g (1 lb) minced beef
1 x 300 g can condensed tomato soup
1 x 425 g can tomatoes, drained
1 teaspoon dried basil
salt and pepper
25 g (8 oz) noodles
1 cup grated Cheddar cheese

Heat the oil in a frying pan, add the onion, garlic and bacon and fry until the onion is softened. Add the carrots and celery and continue frying for 3 minutes. Stir in the beef and brown well, then add the soup, tomatoes, basil and salt and pepper to taste. Cook gently for about 15 minutes.

Meanwhile, cook the noodles in boiling salted water until tender. Drain well. Add the noodles to the beef mixture and fold together, then turn into a casserole. Sprinkle the cheese over the top. Cook in a preheated moderate oven, 180°C (350°F), for 30 minutes.

Serves 4

Beef Olives

1 kg (2 lb) piece of beef topside, cut into 6 slices
salt and pepper
1 teaspoon dried thyme
12 thin slices of smoked ham
30 g (1 oz) butter
1 tablespoon oil
1 onion, chopped
375 ml can stout or beer
thyme sprigs to garnish (optional)

Pound the beef slices until they are thin, then cut each slice in half to make 12 slices, each about 12.5 x 9 cm (5 x 3½ inches). Rub each slice with a little seasoning and thyme, then place a slice of ham on each and trim to fit; reserve any trimmings. Roll up and secure with string.

Melt the butter with the oil in a flameproof casserole. Add the beef rolls and brown on all sides. Remove and set aside.

Add the onion to the casserole with any ham trimmings and fry until softened. Return the beef rolls to the casserole and pour over the stout. Bring to the boil, then cover and transfer to a preheated moderate oven, 180°C (350°F). Cook for 1 hour or until the beef rolls are tender. Remove the string. Garnish with thyme sprigs and serve with carrots, if liked.

Serves 4 to 6

Beef and Spinach Bake

750 g (1½ lb) spinach
1 tablespoon oil
1 large onion, finely chopped
500 g (1 lb) minced beef
250 g (8 oz) mushrooms, sliced
⅔ cup sour cream
½ teaspoon dried oregano
½ teaspoon dried basil
½ teaspoon dried thyme
1 cup grated Cheddar cheese
1 cup grated Parmesan cheese
salt and pepper

Cook the spinach, with just the water clinging to the leaves after washing, until tender. Drain well, pressing out all excess water. Chop the spinach.

Heat the oil in a frying pan. Add the onion and fry until softened. Add the beef and fry until well browned. Stir in the mushrooms and fry for a further 5 minutes. Remove from the heat and drain off all the fat from the pan. Add the chopped spinach, cream, herbs, half the Cheddar and half the Parmesan. Mix well, adding salt and pepper to taste, then turn into a casserole.

Sprinkle the remaining cheeses over the top. Bake in a preheated moderate oven, 180°C (350°F), for 25 minutes.

Serves 4

Lemon Beef Stew

1 tablespoon oil
1 kg (2 lb) beef chuck steak, cut into cubes
2 large onions, chopped
2 lemons, peeled and chopped
1 medium green pepper, cored, seeded and cut into rings
1 x 425 g can tomatoes
2 teaspoons Worcestershire sauce
salt and pepper

Pour the oil into a shallow baking dish and add the beef and onions. Put into a preheated hot oven, 230°C (450°F), and cook for 30 minutes or until the beef is browned on all sides, stirring frequently.

Reduce the heat to moderate, 180°C (350°F). Cover the meat with the chopped lemons and green pepper rings. Mix together the tomatoes with their juice, Worcestershire sauce and salt and pepper to taste and pour over the top. Return to the oven and cook for a further 1½ hours or until the meat is tender. If necessary, add a little water to the dish if it seems too dry during the cooking.

Serves 4

Oxtail Casserole

¼ cup plain flour
salt and pepper
2 oxtails, chopped into pieces
3 tablespoons brandy
1 onion, chopped
2 carrots, chopped
1 bouquet garni
1¼ cups red wine (approximately)
2 cups beef stock or water (approximately)

Season the flour and use to coat the oxtail pieces. Place in a casserole and cook in a preheated very hot oven, 230°C (450°F), for 30 minutes, turning frequently.

Pour off all the fat from the casserole. Warm the brandy, pour over the oxtail pieces and set alight. When the flames have died down, add the onion, carrots, bouquet garni, wine and stock or water.

Lower the oven temperature to moderate, 180°C (350°F), and cook for 4 hours or until the oxtail is tender. Stir during cooking and add more liquid as necessary. Discard the bouquet garni.

Serves 4 to 6

Daube de Boeuf

1 large onion, sliced
2 large carrots, sliced
1¼ cups dry white wine
2 cloves garlic, crushed
1 bay leaf
1 teaspoon dried thyme
salt and pepper
1.5 kg (3 lb) lean chuck steak, cubed
¼ cup flour
250 g (8 oz) bacon rashers, derinded and diced
2 teaspoons finely chopped orange rind
2 x 425 g cans tomatoes, drained and chopped
185 g (6 oz) mushrooms, sliced
12 black olives
⅔ cup stock

Mix together the onion, carrots, wine, garlic, bay leaf, thyme and seasoning in a shallow dish. Add the beef cubes. Leave to marinate in the refrigerator overnight.

Drain the beef, reserving the marinade, and pat dry with kitchen paper. Season the flour and use to coat the beef cubes.

Put about one third of the bacon strips in a flameproof casserole. Spoon over half the marinade, then add half the beef cubes. Sprinkle with half the orange rind, then add half the tomatoes and mushrooms.

Repeat the layers, then top with the black olives and the remaining bacon strips. Pour over the stock.

Bring to the boil on top of the stove, then transfer to a preheated moderate oven, 160°C (325°F), and cook for 4 hours or until tender. Discard the bay leaf.

Serves 6 to 8

Mexican Chilli-Pasta Casserole

2 tablespoons oil
1 medium onion, chopped
500 g (1 lb) minced beef
1 x 425 g can tomatoes
2 tablespoons tomato paste
1 medium green pepper, cored, seeded and diced
1 tablespoon chilli seasoning
salt and pepper
250 g (8 oz) pasta shells
1 x 440 g can red kidney beans, drained
1 cup grated mature Cheddar cheese

Heat the oil in a frying pan, add the onion and fry until softened. Add the beef and brown well, then stir in the tomatoes with their juice, tomato paste, green pepper, chilli seasoning and salt and pepper to taste. Simmer for 15 minutes.

Meanwhile, cook the pasta shells in boiling salted water until tender. Drain well.

Mix the kidney beans into the chilli mixture, then fold in the pasta shells. Turn into a casserole and sprinkle the cheese over the top. Cook in a preheated moderate oven, 180°C (350°F), for 30 minutes.

Serves 4

Gingered Beef

¼ cup plain flour
1 teaspoon ground ginger
salt and pepper
1 kg (2 lb) lean stewing beef, cut into 2.5 cm (1 inch) cubes
3 bacon rashers, derinded and diced
1 large onion, chopped
1 clove garlic, crushed
375 g (12 oz) tomatoes, skinned and chopped
2 tablespoons tomato paste
1¼ cups beef stock
2 tablespoons soy sauce
chopped parsley to garnish

Mix together the flour, ginger and a little salt and pepper, then use to coat the beef cubes. Fry the bacon in a frying pan until it is crisp and has rendered most of its fat. Remove the bacon with a slotted spoon and discard.

Add the beef to the bacon fat in the pan and fry until browned on all sides. Transfer to a casserole.

Add the onion and garlic to the pan and fry until softened. Stir in the tomatoes, tomato paste, beef stock, soy sauce and salt and pepper to taste. Pour into the casserole, cover and cook in a preheated moderate oven, 180°C (350°F), for 2½ to 3 hours or until the beef is tender. Garnish with chopped parsley.
Serves 4

*Illustrated above:
Gingered beef;
Beef casseroled with horseradish (page 28).*

Beef Casseroled with Horseradish

¼ cup plain flour
salt and pepper
1-1.25 kg (2-2½ lb) piece of beef topside
1 tablespoon beef dripping
4 tablespoons horseradish sauce
1 cup water
4 small potatoes, halved
4 medium carrots, sliced
4 button onions

Season the flour and use to coat the beef. Melt the dripping in a flameproof casserole, add the beef and brown on all sides. Spread the horseradish sauce all over the beef and pour in the water. Cover tightly and cook in a preheated moderate oven, 160°C (325°F), for 2½ hours.

Add the vegetables to the casserole with salt and pepper to taste. Re-cover the casserole and cook for a further 1 hour or until the meat and vegetables are tender.
Serves 4

Illustrated on page 27.

Beef Stroganoff Casserole

30 g (1 oz) butter
1 kg (2 lb) lean stewing beef, cut into strips
1 tablespoon oil
1 onion, sliced
250 g (8 oz) mushrooms, sliced
2 tablespoons plain flour
⅔ cup beef stock
⅔ cup sour cream
1 tablespoon tomato paste
salt and pepper
chopped parsley to garnish

Melt the butter in a frying pan, add the beef strips and fry, turning, until evenly browned. Remove the beef strips from the pan with a slotted spoon and place in a casserole.

Add the oil to the frying pan and heat, then add the onion and mushrooms and fry until the onion is softened. Sprinkle over the flour and cook, stirring, for 2 minutes. Gradually stir in the stock. Remove from the heat and stir in the cream, tomato paste and salt and pepper to taste. Pour this mixture into the casserole and stir well.

Cover tightly and cook in a preheated moderate oven, 160°C (325°F), for 1 hour or until the beef is tender. Garnish with chopped parsley.
Serves 4

Beef Carbonnade

60 g (2 oz) beef dripping
1 kg (2 lb) chuck steak, cubed
2 onions, sliced
1 tablespoon plain flour
375 ml can beer
1¼ cups stock or water
salt and pepper
1 bouquet garni
pinch of grated nutmeg
pinch of sugar
1½ teaspoons wine vinegar

Melt the dripping in a flameproof casserole. Add the steak cubes, in batches, and brown on all sides. Remove from the casserole.

Add the onions to the casserole and fry until golden brown. Sprinkle over the flour and cook, stirring, for 2 minutes. Gradually stir in the beer and stock or water and bring to the boil. Add salt and pepper to taste, the bouquet garni, nutmeg, sugar and vinegar. Return the meat to the casserole and stir well.

Cover tightly and cook in a preheated moderate oven, 160°C (325°F), for 2 hours or until the meat is tender. Discard the bouquet garni before serving.
Serves 4

VEAL

Braised Sweetbreads

500 g (1 lb) calf's sweetbreads
30 g (1 oz) butter
1 medium onion, finely chopped
1 large carrot, finely chopped
1 celery stick, finely chopped
4 slices cooked ham, cut into strips
⅔ cup stock
⅔ cup dry white wine
salt and pepper

Blanch the sweetbreads in boiling water for 5 minutes. Drain, then remove ducts and skin and slice.

Melt the butter in a flameproof casserole. Add the onion, carrot, celery and ham and cook until the onion is softened. Stir in the stock, wine and salt and pepper to taste and bring to the boil. Arrange the sweetbreads on top of the vegetables, cover and cook in a preheated moderately hot oven, 190°C (375°F), for 30 minutes.

Serves 4

Golden-Top Casserole

500 g (1 lb) boned veal shoulder, cubed
500 g (1 lb) boned pork chump (escalope), cubed
stock or water
250 g (8 oz) noodles
salt and pepper
1 x 300 g can condensed cream of chicken soup
3 cups grated Cheddar cheese
1 x 310 g can sweetcorn, drained
1 cup fresh breadcrumbs

Put the veal and pork in a saucepan, add stock or water to cover and bring to the boil, skimming off the scum that rises to the surface. Simmer for 45 minutes.

Meanwhile, cook the noodles in boiling salted water until tender. Drain and mix with the soup, 2 cups of the cheese and salt and pepper to taste.

Drain the veal and pork and add to the noodle mixture. Stir well and turn into a casserole.

Spread the sweetcorn over the meat and noodle mixture. Combine the breadcrumbs with the remaining cheese and scatter over the top. Cook in a preheated moderate oven, 180°C (350°F), for 20 to 30 minutes or until the top is browned.

Serves 4

Braised sweetbreads;
Veal goulash (page 32);
Golden-top casserole.

Veal Goulash

45 g (1½ oz) butter
2 streaky bacon rashers, derinded and diced
1 medium onion, chopped
125 g (4 oz) mushrooms, sliced
1 kg (2 lb) boned veal shoulder, cubed
½ teaspoon paprika
1¼ cups sour cream
⅔ cup beef stock or water
salt and pepper
paprika to garnish

Melt the butter in a frying pan, add the bacon and onion and fry until golden. Stir in the mushrooms and fry for a further 5 minutes. Transfer with a slotted spoon to a casserole.

Add the veal to the frying pan and brown on all sides. As the veal cubes brown, transfer to the casserole.

Sprinkle the paprika into the fat remaining in the frying pan and cook, stirring, for 2 minutes. Stir in the sour cream, stock or water and salt and pepper to taste. Pour into the casserole and stir well. Cover the casserole and cook in a preheated moderate oven, 160°C (325°F), for 1 hour or until tender. Sprinkle with paprika to garnish.
Serves 4

Illustrated on page 30.

Veal Parmesan

½ cup dry breadcrumbs
¼ cup grated Parmesan cheese
salt and pepper
500 g (1 lb) veal escalopes, cut into serving portions
1 egg, beaten
45 g (1½ oz) butter, melted
2 tablespoons olive oil
1 onion, thinly sliced
500 g (1 lb) tomatoes, skinned and chopped
2 tablespoons tomato paste
½ teaspoon sugar
½ teaspoon dried oregano
chopped parsley to garnish

Mix together the breadcrumbs, cheese and salt and pepper to taste. Dip the veal into the beaten egg, then coat with the cheese mixture.

Pour the melted butter into a baking dish and arrange the veal in the dish, in one layer, turning them to coat with the melted butter. Cook in a preheated moderately hot oven, 200°C (400°F), for 20 minutes. Turn the veal and cook for 15 minutes.

Meanwhile, heat the oil in a saucepan and fry the onion until softened. Add the tomatoes, tomato paste, sugar, oregano and salt and pepper to taste and stir well. Simmer until the sauce is well reduced.

Pour the tomato sauce over the veal and heat through in the oven for 5 to 10 minutes before serving, garnished with chopped parsley.
Serves 4

Veal with Orange

30 g (1 oz) butter
1 tablespoon oil
750 g (1½ lb) shoulder veal, cubed
1 onion, sliced
3 tablespoons plain flour
1¼ cups chicken stock
⅔ cup orange juice
salt and pepper
2 oranges, peeled and sliced
watercress to garnish

Melt the butter with the oil in a frying pan. Add the veal cubes and brown on all sides. Transfer with a slotted spoon to a casserole.

Add the onion to the pan and fry until golden brown. Add to the casserole.

Stir the flour into the fat remaining in the pan and cook for 3 minutes. Gradually stir in the stock and orange juice and bring to the boil. Season with salt and pepper to taste. Pour over the veal cubes. Arrange the orange slices, overlapping, on top.

Cook in a preheated moderate oven, 180°C (350°F), for 1½ to 2 hours or until the veal is tender. Garnish with watercress.

Serves 4

Meatball Casserole

1 kg (2 lb) minced veal
4 tablespoons fresh breadcrumbs
2 tablespoons grated Parmesan cheese
2 tablespoons chopped parsley
salt and pepper
1 egg, beaten
30 g (1 oz) butter
1 tablespoon oil
1 onion, chopped
2 celery sticks, chopped
1 apple, peeled, cored and diced
$2/3$ cup stock
$2/3$ cup red wine
4 tablespoons sweet pickle
2 tablespoons chopped sultanas
chopped parsley to garnish

Mix together the veal, breadcrumbs, cheese, parsley and salt and pepper to taste. Bind the mixture with the egg. Shape into meatballs about the size of walnuts.

Melt the butter with the oil in a frying pan. Add the meatballs, in batches, and brown on all sides, then transfer to a casserole.

Add the onion, celery and apple to the frying pan and fry until the onion is softened. Stir in the stock, wine, pickle and sultanas and bring to the boil. Simmer for 10 minutes.

Pour the sauce over the meatballs. Cover and cook in a preheated moderately hot oven, 190°C (375°F), for 30 minutes or until the meatballs are cooked through. Garnish with chopped parsley.
Serves 4

Roman Veal Casserole

¼ cup plain flour
salt and pepper
750 g (1½ lb) veal escalopes, cut into serving portions
30 g (1 oz) butter
1 tablespoon olive oil
250 g (8 oz) mushrooms, sliced
1 clove garlic, crushed
1 x 400 g can tomatoes, drained and chopped
⅔ cup Marsala
1 teaspoon dried basil
½ teaspoon dried oregano
chopped parsley to garnish

Season the flour and use to coat the veal. Melt the butter with the oil in a flameproof casserole. Add the veal and brown on all sides, then remove and set aside.

Add the mushrooms and garlic to the casserole and fry for 3 minutes. Stir in the tomatoes, Marsala, herbs and seasoning to taste. Bring to the boil.

Return the veal to the casserole and mix into the sauce. Cover and cook in a preheated moderate oven, 160°C (325°F), for 45 minutes. Serve garnished with parsley.

Serves 4

LAMB

Lamb Stew

60 g (2 oz) butter
8 lamb chops, trimmed
1 large onion, chopped
1 tablespoon plain flour
1 x 411 g can consommé
1 bouquet garni
salt and pepper
1 kg (2 lb) potatoes, cut into 4 cm (1½ inch) chunks
chopped parsley to garnish

Melt the butter in a flameproof casserole. Add the chops and brown on both sides, then remove and set aside. Add the onion to the casserole and fry until softened. Sprinkle over the flour and stir well, then return the chops to the casserole.

Pour over the consommé and add the bouquet garni with salt and pepper to taste. Bring to the boil, then cover and cook in a preheated moderate oven, 180°C (350°F), for 1 hour.

Stir in the potatoes, re-cover the casserole and continue cooking for 45 minutes or until the chops are cooked and the potatoes tender. Remove the bouquet garni. Garnish with parsley before serving.

Serves 4

Lamb stew; Kidney ragoût; Lamb ratatouille (page 38).

Kidney Ragoût

3 tablespoons plain flour
salt and pepper
30 g (1 oz) butter
250 g (8 oz) streaky bacon rashers, derinded and diced
12 lambs' kidneys, sliced
1 large onion, finely chopped
1 clove garlic, crushed
1 red pepper, cored, seeded and diced
2 tomatoes, skinned, seeded and chopped
2/3 cup beef stock
5 tablespoons red wine
triangles of fried bread to garnish

Season the flour and use to coat the kidney slices. Melt the butter in a frying pan and fry the bacon until crisp. Remove with a slotted spoon and place in a casserole.

Add the kidney slices to the frying pan and brown on all sides. Transfer to the casserole.

Add the onion, garlic and red pepper to the frying pan and fry until the onion is softened. Stir in the tomatoes, stock and wine and bring to the boil, then pour into the casserole and mix well. Cover and cook in a preheated moderate oven, 180°C (350°F), for 30 minutes or until the kidneys are tender. Garnish with triangles of fried bread before serving.

Serves 4

Lamb Ratatouille

1 large eggplant, halved lengthways and sliced
salt and pepper
4 tablespoons olive oil (approximately)
1 kg (2 lb) boned shoulder of lamb, cubed
1 large onion, sliced
750 g (1½ lb) zucchini, sliced
½ red and ½ green pepper, cored, seeded and sliced
1 x 400 g can tomatoes
1 teaspoon dried basil

Sprinkle the eggplant slices with salt and leave to drain for 30 minutes. Rinse and pat dry.

Heat 3 tablespoons of the oil in a flameproof casserole. Add the lamb cubes and brown on all sides, then remove and set aside.

Add the onion to the casserole, with the remaining oil if necessary, and fry until softened. Add the eggplant, zucchini, red or green pepper, tomatoes with their juice, basil and salt and pepper to taste. Cover and cook for 10 minutes.

Stir the lamb cubes into the vegetable mixture. Re-cover and cook in a preheated moderate oven, 180°C (350°F), for 1 hour or until tender.

Serves 4 to 6

Illustrated on page 37.

Orange Lamb Casserole

1 large onion, sliced
2 teaspoon dried marjoram
1 orange
1.75 kg (4 lb) loin of lamb, in one piece
salt and pepper
1¼ cups dry white wine or stock
⅔ cup orange juice
1 tablespoon orange marmalade

Put the onion slices in a greased casserole and sprinkle with the marjoram. Pare the rind from the orange in strips and scatter over the onion. Peel and slice the orange.

Rub the lamb with salt and pepper and place in the casserole. Arrange the orange slices over the meat. Pour in the wine or stock and orange juice.

Cover and cook in a preheated moderate oven, 160°C (325°F), for 2 to 2½ hours or until the meat is tender.

Transfer the meat to a warmed serving dish. Arrange the orange slices on top and keep hot.

Strain the cooking liquid into a saucepan. Skim off the fat and boil until reduced and thickened. Stir in the marmalade and adjust the seasoning. Serve with the lamb.

Serves 4

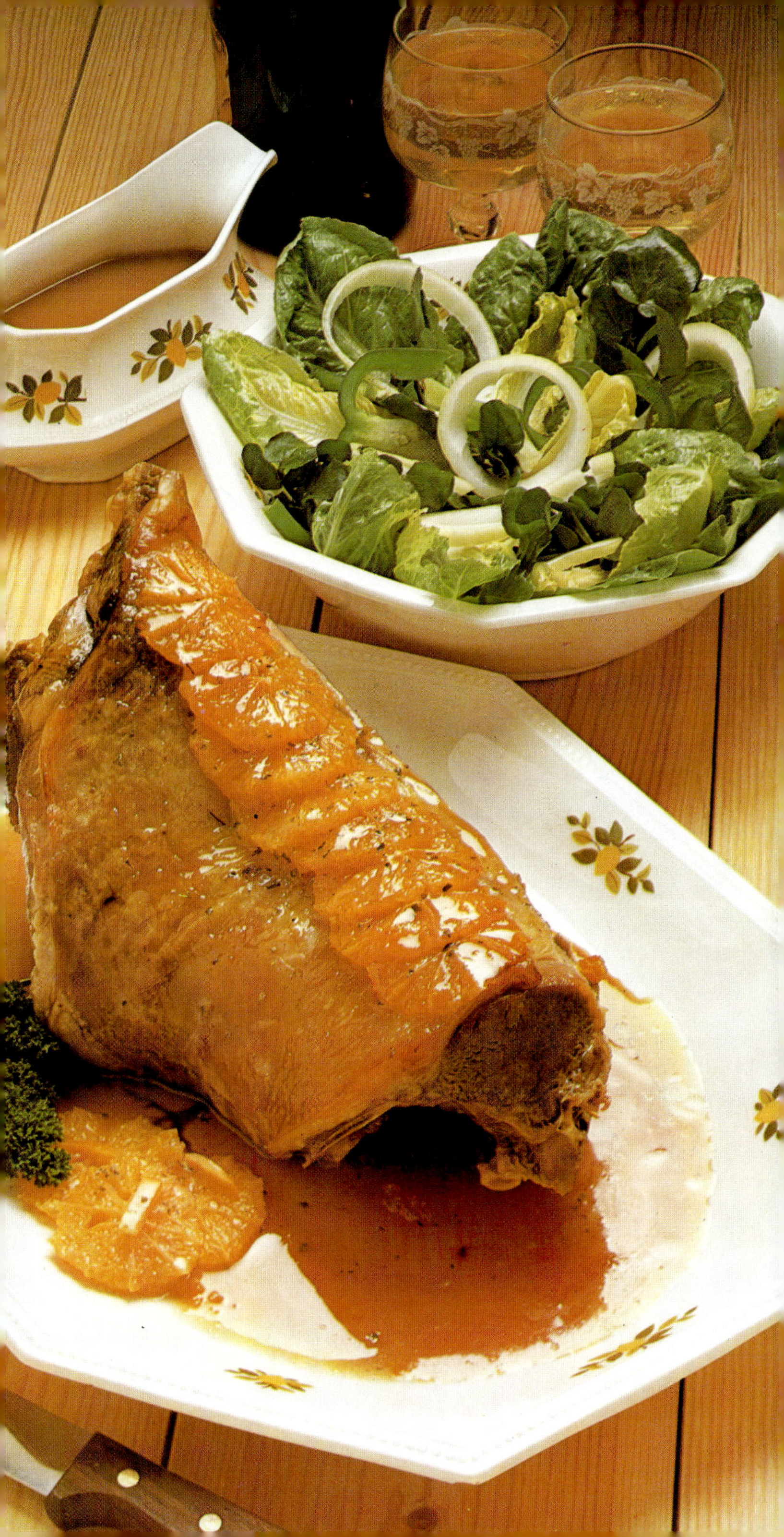

Moussaka

2 medium eggplant, sliced
salt and pepper
6 tablespoons olive oil (approximately)
1 large onion, chopped
1 clove garlic, finely chopped
750 g (1½ lb) cooked lamb, finely chopped
250 g (8 oz) tomatoes, skinned and chopped
2 tablespoons chopped parsley
grated nutmeg
30 g (1 oz) butter
¼ cup plain flour
1¼ cups milk
1 egg yolk
parsley sprigs to garnish

Sprinkle the eggplant slices with salt and leave to drain for 30 minutes. Rinse and pat dry with kitchen paper. Heat a little of the olive oil in a frying pan. Fry the eggplant slices, in batches, until golden brown on both sides, adding more oil as necessary.

Add the onion and garlic to the pan, with more oil if necessary, and fry until softened. Stir in the lamb, tomatoes, parsley, salt, pepper and nutmeg to taste. Cook for 5 minutes.

Make alternate layers of eggplant and lamb in a casserole, beginning and ending with eggplant slices.

Melt the butter in a saucepan. Add the flour and cook, stirring, for 1 minute. Gradually stir in the milk and bring to the boil. Simmer, stirring, until thickened. Season with salt, pepper and nutmeg to taste. Cool slightly, then beat in the egg yolk.

Pour the sauce over the eggplant slices. Cook in a preheated moderate oven, 180°C (350°F), for 45 minutes. Garnish with parsley.
Serves 4

Liver and Bacon Hotpot

1 large onion, sliced
2 medium cooking apples, peeled, cored and sliced
125 g (4 oz) mushrooms, sliced
250 g (8 oz) bacon rashers, derinded
750 g (1½ lb) lamb's liver, sliced
salt and pepper
½ x 411 g can consommé
1 x 400 g can tomatoes, drained and chopped
chopped parsley to garnish

Spread one third of the onion over the bottom of a greased casserole. Add one third of the apple slices, then one third of the mushrooms and bacon, then half the liver. Season well. Continue making layers in this way. Pour in the consommé and spread the tomatoes over the top. Cover tightly and cook in a preheated moderate oven, 180°C (350°F), for 1½ hours. Serve garnished with chopped parsley.

Serves 4

Lamb Chops with Apples

30 g (1 oz) butter
1 tablespoon oil
1 large onion, thinly sliced
2 large cooking apples, peeled, cored and sliced
2 tablespoons raisins
2 tablespoons brown sugar
salt and pepper
8 or 12 lamb chops, trimmed
2/3 cup dry cider

Melt the butter with the oil in a frying pan. Add the onion and fry until softened. Remove the onion from the pan with a slotted spoon and spread half over the bottom of a casserole. Cover with half the apple slices and sprinkle with half the raisins, half the sugar and salt and pepper to taste.

Put the chops in the frying pan and brown on both sides. Drain the chops and place in the casserole. Cover with the rest of the onion and apples and sprinkle with the remaining raisins, sugar, salt and pepper. Pour in the cider.

Cover the casserole and cook in a preheated moderate oven, 180°C (350°F), for 1½ hours or until the chops are very tender.
Serves 4

Lamb, Pork and Potato Casserole

30 g (1 oz) butter
750 g (1½ lb) potatoes, sliced
500 g (1 lb) boned shoulder of lamb, cubed
500 g (1 lb) boned shoulder of pork, cubed
2 onions, chopped
salt and pepper
⅔ cup dry white wine

Grease a casserole with half the butter. Make a layer of half the potato slices on the bottom, then add the lamb, pork and onions in layers, sprinkling each layer with a little salt and pepper. Pour over the wine. Arrange the remaining potato slices on top and dot with the remaining butter. Cover and cook in a preheated moderately hot oven, 190°C (375°F), for 1½ hours.

Uncover the casserole and continue cooking for 30 minutes or until the potato topping is golden brown.
Serves 4 to 6

Lamb with Mushrooms and Tomatoes

45 g (1½ oz) butter
250 g (8 oz)
　mushrooms,
　chopped
1 tablespoon flour
⅔ cup milk
⅔ cup chicken stock
2 tablespoons
　medium sherry
salt and pepper
750 g (1½ lb)
　cooked lamb,
　chopped
500 g (1 lb) tomatoes,
　skinned and sliced
½ cup fresh
　breadcrumbs
¼ cup grated mature
　Cheddar cheese
2 tablespoons
　chopped parsley

Melt the butter in a saucepan. Add the mushrooms and fry for 3 minutes. Sprinkle over the flour and cook, stirring, for 2 minutes. Gradually stir in the milk and stock. Bring to the boil and simmer, stirring, until thickened. Add the sherry and salt and pepper to taste, then fold in the lamb. Turn into a greased baking dish.

　Arrange the tomato slices over the lamb mixture. Combine the breadcrumbs, cheese and parsley and sprinkle over the top. Bake in a preheated moderate oven, 180°C (350°F), for 30 minutes or until the top is golden brown.

Serves 4

Haricot of Lamb

2 cups dried white haricot beans, soaked overnight
1 onion, stuck with 4 cloves
1 bay leaf
salt and pepper
3 tablespoons plain flour
1 kg (2 lb) boned lamb shoulder, cut into 2.5 cm (1 inch) cubes
3 tablespoons oil
2 cloves garlic, finely chopped
1 large onion, chopped
1 x 400 g can tomatoes, drained
2 cups chicken stock (approximately)
1 tablespoon lemon juice
1 teaspoon dried thyme
¼ cup dry breadcrumbs
15 g (½ oz) butter, melted

Drain the beans and put them in a saucepan with the onion stuck with cloves, the bay leaf and 1 teaspoon salt. Pour over water to cover and bring to the boil. Simmer gently for 1 hour or until the beans are tender.

Meanwhile, season the flour and use to coat the lamb cubes. Heat the oil in a flameproof casserole, add the garlic and chopped onion and fry until softened. Add the lamb cubes and brown on all sides. Stir in the tomatoes, stock, lemon juice and thyme and bring to the boil. Cover and cook in a preheated moderate oven, 180°C (350°F), for 1 hour.

Drain the beans, discarding the onion and bay leaf, and add to the casserole. Stir well. Add a little more stock if necessary. Re-cover the casserole and cook for a further 1 hour or until the lamb is tender.

Mix together the breadcrumbs and butter. Uncover the casserole and sprinkle over the breadcrumbs. Cook for 15 to 20 minutes or until the topping is golden brown.

Serves 4 to 6

PORK

Plummy Pork Chops

15 g (½ oz) butter
1 tablespoon oil
4 or 8 pork chops
500 g (1 lb) plums, stoned
sugar
½ teaspoon ground allspice
3 tablespoons water
⅔ cup red wine (approximately)
salt and pepper
watercress to garnish

Melt the butter with the oil in a frying pan. Add the chops and brown on both sides, then drain and place in a shallow casserole.

Put the plums, sugar to taste, allspice and water in a saucepan and cook gently until the plums are very soft. Allow to cool slightly, then rub through a sieve or purée in an electric blender. Mix in the red wine and salt and pepper to taste, then pour over the chops. Add more red wine if necessary so the chops are just covered.

Cover and cook in a preheated moderate oven, 180°C (350°F), for 45 minutes or until the chops are tender. Serve garnished with watercress.
Serves 4

Plummy pork chops; Pork and French beans; Pork in mushroom sauce (page 48).

Pork and Green Beans

3 tablespoons plain flour
½ teaspoon ground ginger
salt and pepper
1 kg (2 lb) boned pork shoulder, trimmed of fat and cut into cubes
30 g (1 oz) butter
2 tablespoons oil
2 onions, thinly sliced
1 clove garlic, crushed
2 cups chicken stock (approximately)
250 g (8 oz) tomatoes, skinned and chopped
350 g (12 oz) green beans, cut into 5 cm (2 inch) lengths

Mix the flour with the ginger and a little salt and pepper, then use to coat the pork cubes. Melt the butter with the oil in a flameproof casserole. Add the onions and garlic and fry until softened. Add the pork cubes and brown on all sides. Stir in enough stock to cover the pork and bring to the boil. Cover the casserole and cook in a preheated moderate oven, 160°C (325°F), for 2½ hours.

Skim any fat from the surface, then stir in the tomatoes. Lay the beans over the top and press down gently so they become moistened with the cooking liquid. Re-cover the casserole and continue cooking for a further 30 minutes.

Serves 4

Pork in Mushroom Sauce

60 g (2 oz) butter
2 tablespoons oil
1 kg (2 lb) pork
   fillet, sliced
1 large onion, sliced
salt and pepper
1¼ cups dry red
   wine
250 g (8 oz)
   mushrooms, sliced
1 tablespoon plain
   flour
1¼ cups cream
chopped chives to
   garnish

Melt the butter with the oil in a frying pan. Add the pork slices and brown on both sides. Remove from the pan with a slotted spoon and place in a flameproof casserole.

Add the onion to the frying pan and fry until softened. Drain and arrange over the pork. Add salt and pepper to taste, and the wine.

Cover and cook in a preheated moderate oven, 180°C (350°F), for 1¼ hours. Stir in the mushrooms and cook for 15 minutes or until the pork is tender.

Mix together the flour and cream and stir into the casserole. Cook gently on top of the stove, stirring, until the liquid has thickened; do not boil. Serve garnished with chives.
Serves 4

Illustrated on page 47.

Barbecued Sparerib Casserole

8 pork sparerib chops
salt and pepper
30 g (1 oz) butter
1 tablespoon oil
1 onion, chopped
1 clove garlic, crushed
1 cup tomato ketchup
   or sauce
1 cup water
4 tablespoons cider
   vinegar
4 tablespoons
   Worcestershire
   sauce
¼ cup brown sugar
1 teaspoon mild chilli
   powder
few drops of Tabasco
   sauce
8 lemon slices

Rub the chops with salt and pepper on both sides. Melt the butter with the oil in a frying pan. Add the chops, in batches, and brown on both sides, then transfer to a baking dish, arranging them in one layer if possible.

Add the onion and garlic to the frying pan and fry until softened. Stir in the ketchup, water, vinegar, Worcestershire sauce, brown sugar, chilli powder and Tabasco sauce and bring to the boil. Simmer for 30 minutes.

Taste the sauce and adjust the seasoning. Place a lemon slice on each pork chop, then pour over the sauce. Bake in a preheated moderate oven, 180°C (350°F), for 1½ hours or until the chops are tender, turning them occasionally.
Serves 4

Chilli Pork

2 tablespoons oil
1 large onion, chopped
1 green pepper, cored, seeded and diced
1 kg (2 lb) pork chump (escalope), cubed
1 x 300 g can condensed tomato soup
2 celery sticks, chopped
1 tablespoon chilli seasoning
1 x 400 g can tomatoes, drained and chopped
1 x 440 g can red kidney beans, drained
salt and pepper

Heat the oil in a flameproof casserole. Add the onion and green pepper and fry until softened. Stir in the pork cubes and brown lightly on all sides. Cover tightly and cook in a preheated moderate oven, 180°C (350°F), for 40 minutes.

Stir in the soup, celery, chilli seasoning and tomatoes. Re-cover the casserole and cook for a further 20 minutes or until the pork is tender. Stir in the kidney beans with salt and pepper to taste. Cook, uncovered, for a further 10 minutes or until the beans are heated through.
Serves 4

Sausage and Bean Casserole

500 g (1 lb) pork sausages
1 large onion, chopped
2 x 440 g cans baked beans
1½ cups finely chopped dried apricots
2 tablespoons brown sugar
1 teaspoon dry mustard
salt and pepper

Prick the sausages all over, then fry in a dry frying pan until they are browned all over and have rendered some of their fat. Remove from the pan, cut into 1 cm (½ inch) slices and set aside.

Pour off all but 2 tablespoons fat from the pan and add the onion. Fry until softened then drain and put into a casserole. Add the sausage slices, baked beans, apricots, sugar and mustard. Mix well and add salt and pepper to taste. Cover and cook in a preheated moderate oven, 180°C (350°F), for 30 to 45 minutes or until heated through.
Serves 4

Cidered Sausages

15 g (½ oz) butter
3 bacon rashers, derinded and diced
500 g (1 lb) pork sausages
2 onions, sliced
1 large carrot, diced
1 green pepper, cored, seeded and diced
3 tablespoons flour
1½ cups dry cider
1 tablespoon Worcestershire sauce
salt and pepper
TOPPING:
½ cup corn meal
½ cup plain flour
2 teaspoons baking powder
pinch of sugar
¼ teaspoon salt
1 egg
30 g (1 oz) margarine, melted
7 tablespoons milk (approximately)

Melt the butter in a frying pan, add the bacon and fry until crisp. Remove with a slotted spoon.

Add the sausages to the pan and brown on all sides, then remove from the pan and cut in half.

Add the onions, carrot and green pepper to the pan and fry until the onions are softened. Sprinkle over the flour and cook, stirring, for 2 minutes. Gradually stir in the cider and Worcestershire sauce and bring to the boil, stirring. Season with salt and pepper to taste.

Return the bacon and sausages to the pan and stir well. Cover and simmer while making the topping.

Mix together the corn meal, flour, baking powder, sugar and salt. Add the egg, margarine and enough milk to make a smooth thick batter.

Pour the sausage mixture into a deep baking dish not more than 20 cm (8 inches) in diameter. Pour the cornbread topping over. Cook in a preheated hot oven, 225°C (425°F), for 15 to 20 minutes.
Serves 4

Ham and Egg Pie

4 medium potatoes
salt and pepper
250 g (8 oz) cooked ham, chopped
6 hard-boiled eggs, sliced
1 cup grated Cheddar cheese
4 spring onions, chopped
1¼ cups sour cream
2 tomatoes, sliced
chopped chives to garnish

Cook the potatoes in boiling, salted water until tender. Drain and slice.

Make alternate layers of potato, ham, eggs and cheese in a greased casserole, sprinkling each layer of egg slices with salt and pepper and chopped spring onions. Begin and end with potato slices. Pour the cream over the top and arrange the tomato slices in a ring around the edge. Bake in a preheated moderate oven, 180°C (350°F), for 30 minutes. Serve garnished with chives.
Serves 4

Pork and Apple Casserole

30 g (1 oz) butter
2 large cooking apples, peeled, cored and sliced
1 large onion, chopped
2 teaspoons sugar
2 teaspoons dried sage
4 or 8 pork chops
salt and pepper
125 g (4 oz) mushrooms, sliced
1 cup dry cider
1 cup fresh breadcrumbs
½ cup grated mature Cheddar cheese

Grease a shallow baking dish with half the butter. Place half the apple slices in the dish and sprinkle with half the onion, sugar and sage. Arrange the chops on top, season with salt and pepper to taste and cover with the mushrooms. Add the remaining apples, onion, sugar and sage. Pour in the cider.

Mix together the breadcrumbs and cheese and sprinkle over the top. Dot with the remaining butter. Cook in a preheated moderately hot oven, 200°C (400°F), for 45 minutes or until the chops are cooked and the top is browned.

Serves 4

Pork Casseroled with Fruit

15 g (½ oz) butter
1 tablespoon oil
4 or 8 pork chops
1 x 425 g can apricot halves
½ x 450 g can pineapple rings
8 prunes, stoned and chopped
2 tablespoons brown sugar
5 tablespoons chicken stock
⅔ cup cream
salt and pepper

Melt the butter with the oil in a frying pan. Add the chops and brown on both sides. Remove the chops from the pan, drain, then arrange in a flameproof casserole.

Drain the apricot halves and pineapple rings, reserving the syrup. Place the fruit, with the prunes, on top of the chops to cover them. Sprinkle with the brown sugar.

Mix the stock with 5 tablespoons each of the apricot and pineapple syrups. Pour into the casserole.

Cover tightly and cook in a preheated moderate oven, 180°C (350°F), for about 1 hour or until the chops are tender.

Transfer the chops to a warmed serving dish, being careful not to dislodge the fruit on top. Keep hot.

Boil the liquid in the casserole until reduced to about ⅔ cup. Skim off any fat, then stir in the cream with salt and pepper to taste. Heat through gently and serve this sauce with the pork.
Serves 4

POULTRY & GAME

Casseroled Pheasant

1 x 1.5 kg (3 lb) pheasant
salt and pepper
60 g (2 oz) butter
1 onion, chopped
2 carrots, diced
1 celery stick, chopped
1¼ cups stock
⅔ cup red wine
1 bay leaf
2 tablespoons redcurrant jelly
parsley sprigs to garnish

Rub the pheasant with seasoning. Melt the butter in a flameproof casserole, add the pheasant and brown on all sides, then remove and set aside.

Add the onion, carrots and celery to the casserole and fry until softened. Stir in the stock, wine and bay leaf and bring to the boil. Return the pheasant to the casserole.

Cover and cook in a preheated moderate oven, 180°C (350°F), for 1¼ hours or until the pheasant is tender. Transfer the pheasant to a warmed serving dish and keep hot. Skim any fat from the cooking liquid, then rub through a sieve or purée in an electric blender. Return to the casserole and boil until well reduced and thickened. Adjust the seasoning and stir in the redcurrant jelly. Serve with the pheasant. Garnish the dish with parsley.
Serves 4

Duckling and Orange Casserole

1 x 2.5 kg (5 lb) duckling, quartered and skinned
30 g (1 oz) butter
1 small onion, finely chopped
⅔ cup orange juice
¼ teaspoon dried tarragon
pinch of dry mustard
2 tablespoons port
4 tablespoons redcurrant jelly
1 orange
salt and pepper
2 teaspoons cornflour

Casseroled pheasant; Duckling and orange casserole; Turkey bake (page 56).

Remove all fat from the duckling quarters, then place them in a flameproof casserole.

Melt the butter in a saucepan, add the onion and fry until softened. Stir in all but 1 tablespoon of the orange juice, the tarragon, mustard, port and redcurrant jelly. Grate the rind from the orange and add to the pan with salt and pepper to taste. Bring to the boil, stirring, then pour over the duckling quarters.

Peel the orange, divide into segments and place on top of the duckling. Cover and cook in a preheated moderate oven, 180°C (350°F), for 1 hour or until the duckling is tender. Transfer the duckling quarters and orange segments to a serving dish and keep hot.

Skim any fat from the surface of the cooking liquid. Dissolve the cornflour in the reserved orange juice and stir into the cooking liquid. Simmer on top of the stove, stirring, until thickened. Serve with the duckling.

Serves 4

Turkey Bake

375 g (12 oz) cooked turkey, chopped
2 medium potatoes, cooked and diced
1 onion, grated
⅔ cup milk
1 egg, beaten
1 teaspoon grated lemon rind
salt and pepper
8 water biscuits, finely crushed
15 g (½ oz) butter, melted

Mix together the turkey, potatoes, onion, milk, egg, lemon rind and salt and pepper to taste. Turn into a greased casserole.

Combine the crushed biscuits and melted butter and sprinkle over the top. Cook in a preheated moderate oven, 180°C (350°F), for about 30 minutes.
Serves 4

Illustrated on page 55.

Rabbit in Cranberry Sauce

4 rabbit joints
1 tablespoon vinegar
¼ cup plain flour
salt and pepper
¼ teaspoon ground allspice
30 g (1 oz) butter
2 tablespoons oil
1 onion, chopped
1 large carrot, diced
1¼ cups chicken stock
1¼ cups dry white wine
1 bay leaf
⅓ cup whole berry cranberry sauce

Soak the rabbit joints overnight in water with the vinegar added. Drain, rinse and pat dry with kitchen paper.

Season the flour with salt and pepper and the allspice and use to coat the rabbit joints. Melt the butter with the oil in a flameproof casserole. Add the rabbit and brown on all sides, then remove.

Add the onion and carrot to the casserole and fry until softened. Stir in the stock and wine and bring to the boil. Return the rabbit to the casserole with the bay leaf. Cover and cook in a preheated moderate oven, 180°C (350°F), for 1½ hours or until tender.

Remove the rabbit pieces from the casserole and keep warm. Boil the cooking liquid until reduced to about 1¼ cups. Strain the liquid and return to the casserole. Stir in the cranberry sauce and adjust seasoning.

Return the rabbit to the casserole and turn to coat with the sauce. Cover and return to the oven for 10 minutes or until heated through.
Serves 4

Rabbit with Mustard Sauce

4 rabbit joints
1 tablespoon vinegar
30 g (1 oz) butter
250 g (8 oz) streaky bacon, derinded and diced
2 onions, chopped
1 tablespoon plain flour
2 cups chicken stock
salt and pepper
1 bouquet garni
⅔ cup cream
2 tablespoons French mustard
chopped parsley to garnish

Soak the rabbit joints overnight in water with the vinegar added. Drain, rinse and pat dry with kitchen paper.

Melt the butter in a flameproof casserole. Add the rabbit pieces and brown on all sides, then remove.

Add the bacon and onions to the casserole and fry until golden brown. Sprinkle over the flour and cook, stirring, for 2 minutes. Gradually stir in the stock and bring to the boil. Season with salt and pepper to taste, then return the rabbit to the casserole and add the bouquet garni.

Cover and cook in a preheated moderate oven, 180°C (350°F), for 1½ hours or until tender.

Remove the rabbit from the casserole. Discard the bouquet garni. Mix the cream with the mustard and stir into the cooking liquid. Heat, stirring, on top of the stove; do not boil. Return the rabbit and reheat. Serve garnished with parsley.
Serves 4

Hunter's Casserole

1¼ cups dry red wine
4 tablespoons olive oil
1 clove garlic, crushed
1 bay leaf
salt and pepper
1 kg (2 lb) boneless hare or rabbit, cut into cubes
30 g (1 oz) butter
2 large carrots, sliced
⅔ cup beef stock
250 g (8 oz) small onions
250 g (8 oz) button mushrooms

Mix together the wine, oil, garlic, bay leaf and salt and pepper in a shallow dish. Add the hare or rabbit and leave to marinate overnight, turning occasionally.

Drain the hare, reserving the marinade, and pat dry with kitchen paper. Melt the butter in a flameproof casserole. Add the hare cubes and brown on all sides. Stir in the reserved marinade, carrots and stock and bring to the boil. Cover and cook in a preheated moderate oven, 180°C (350°F), for 2 hours.

Meanwhile, blanch the onions in boiling water for 5 minutes, then drain and peel, when cool enough to handle.

Add the onions and mushrooms to the casserole and stir well. Cook, uncovered, for a further 30 minutes or until the hare is tender. Discard the bay leaf before serving.
Serves 4

Japanese Chicken Casserole

- ⅔ cup chicken stock
- 5 tablespoons dry sherry
- 3 tablespoons soy sauce
- 1 teaspoon sugar
- 8 chicken pieces, skinned
- ¼ cup cornflour
- 1 teaspoon ground ginger
- salt and pepper
- 4 tablespoons oil
- 2 canned water chestnuts, drained and sliced
- 4 spring onions, chopped

Mix together the stock, sherry, soy sauce and sugar in a shallow dish. Add the chicken pieces and turn to coat. Leave to marinate in the refrigerator overnight.

Drain the chicken pieces, reserving the marinade, and pat dry with kitchen paper. Mix the cornflour, ginger, salt and pepper together. Heat the oil in a frying pan, add the chicken pieces and brown on all sides.

Cover the bottom of a greased flameproof casserole with the water chestnuts and spring onions. Drain the chicken pieces and place them on top. Pour over the marinade and bring to the boil. Cover and cook in a preheated moderate oven, 180°C (350°F), for about 1 hour or until the chicken is tender.

Serves 4

Coq au Vin

125 g (4 oz) salt pork, diced
30 g (1 oz) butter
4 chicken quarters
250 g (8 oz) small onions
1 clove garlic, crushed
2 tablespoons plain flour
2½ cups dry red wine
salt and pepper
250 g (8 oz) button mushrooms
⅔ cup chicken stock (approximately)
1 bouquet garni
chopped parsley to garnish

Blanch the salt pork in boiling water for 5 minutes, then drain well. Melt the butter in a frying pan and fry the pork until beginning to crisp. Remove with a slotted spoon and place in a casserole.

Add the chicken quarters to the pan and brown on all sides, then transfer to the casserole.

Add the onions and garlic to the pan and cook gently until they are beginning to soften and brown. Add to the casserole.

Pour off all but about 2 tablespoons of fat from the pan and stir in the flour. Cook, stirring, for 2 minutes. Gradually stir in the wine, bring to the boil, then simmer, stirring, until thickened. Season with salt and pepper to taste and stir in the mushrooms.

Pour the sauce over the chicken in the casserole, adding enough stock to cover the chicken. Add the bouquet garni, cover and cook in a preheated moderately hot oven, 190°C (375°F), for about 1 hour or until the chicken is tender. Remove the bouquet garni and serve sprinkled with chopped parsley.

Serves 4

Arroz con Pollo

60 g (2 oz) butter
3 tablespoons olive oil
1 clove garlic, crushed
8 chicken pieces
2½ cups long-grain rice
6 cups chicken stock
1 teaspoon turmeric
salt and pepper
60 g (2 oz) chorizo or garlic sausage, chopped
1 red pepper, cored, seeded and diced
parsley sprigs to garnish

Melt the butter with the oil in a flameproof casserole. Add the garlic and chicken pieces and brown on all sides. Remove the chicken pieces.

Add the rice to the casserole and stir well to mix with the fat. Fry until golden, stirring, then stir in the stock, turmeric and salt and pepper to taste. Bring to the boil.

Add the chorizo or garlic sausage and red pepper and mix well. Return the chicken pieces to the casserole and bury in the rice mixture. Cover and cook in a preheated moderate oven, 180°C (350°F), for about 1 hour or until the chicken is tender and the rice has absorbed the liquid. Serve garnished with parsley.

Serves 4

Curried Chicken Casserole

60 g (2 oz) butter
2 large onions, finely chopped
1 clove garlic, crushed
1 green chilli, seeded and finely chopped
2.5 cm (1 inch) piece fresh root ginger, peeled and finely chopped
1 teaspoon turmeric
½ teaspoon ground cardamom
1 teaspoon ground coriander
1 teaspoon ground cumin
1 teaspoon salt
1½ cups plain yogurt
4 chicken quarters, skinned

Melt the butter in a flameproof casserole, add the onions and fry until softened. Stir in the garlic, chilli, ginger, turmeric, cardamom, coriander, cumin and salt and cook, stirring, for 5 minutes. Stir in the yogurt, then add the chicken pieces to the casserole and spoon the spice mixture over them. Cover and cook in a preheated moderate oven, 160°C (325°F), for 1½ hours or until the chicken is tender.

Serves 4

Spring Chicken Casserole

3 tablespoons plain flour
¼ teaspoon paprika
salt and pepper
8 chicken pieces
60 g (2 oz) butter
8 small new carrots, scraped
12 small onions
1 celery stick, cut into 5 cm (2 inch) strips
2 cups boiling chicken stock
1 bouquet garni
3 tablespoons cream

Mix the flour with the paprika and a little salt and pepper, then use to coat the chicken pieces. Melt the butter in a frying pan and brown the chicken pieces on all sides, then transfer to a casserole.

Add the carrots, onions and celery to the fat in the pan and fry until just golden. Add to the chicken. Pour over the stock and add the bouquet garni. Cover and cook in a preheated moderate oven, 180°C (350°F), for about 1¼ hours or until the chicken and vegetables are tender. Discard the bouquet garni. Stir in the cream just before serving.

Serves 4

Welsh Chicken Casserole

500 g (1 lb) leeks
500 g (1 lb) cooked chicken meat, cut into strips
75 g (2½ oz) butter
½ cup plain flour
1¼ cups chicken stock
1¼ cups milk
¼ teaspoon dry mustard
salt and pepper
¾ cup grated Cheddar cheese
¼ cup dry breadcrumbs

Halve the leeks crossways, then cut into quarters lengthways. Place in a greased casserole and arrange the chicken on top.

Melt 60 g (2 oz) of the butter in a saucepan. Add the flour and cook, stirring, for 2 minutes. Gradually stir in the stock and milk. Bring to the boil, then simmer, stirring, until thickened. Add the mustard, salt and pepper to taste and the cheese and stir until melted. Pour this sauce over the chicken and leeks.

Melt the remaining butter and mix with the breadcrumbs. Scatter over the top of the casserole. Cook in a preheated moderate oven, 180°C (350°F), for 30 minutes.
Serves 4

Illustrated above: Welsh chicken casserole; Grapefruit chicken (page 64).

Grapefruit Chicken

8 half chicken
  breasts, skinned
salt and pepper
30 g (1 oz) butter
1 tablespoon oil
1 large onion, sliced
1 teaspoon grated
  grapefruit rind
¾ cup fresh
  grapefruit juice
3 tablespoons honey
grapefruit segments
  to garnish

Rub the chicken breasts with salt and pepper. Melt the butter with the oil in a frying pan and fry the chicken pieces until browned on all sides. Transfer to a casserole.

Add the onion to the fat remaining in the pan and fry until softened. Arrange the onion over the chicken.

Mix together the grapefruit rind and juice, honey and salt and pepper to taste, then pour over the chicken pieces. Cover and cook in a preheated moderate oven, 180°C (350°F), for 45 minutes or until the chicken is cooked through. Serve garnished with grapefruit segments.
Serves 4 to 6

Illustrated on page 63.

Smothered Chicken

½ cup plain flour
salt and pepper
8 chicken pieces
60 g (2 oz) butter
1 onion, finely
  chopped
1 small carrot, diced
1 small celery stick,
  finely chopped
2 cups chicken stock
5 tablespoons cream

Season half the flour and use to coat the chicken pieces. Melt the butter in a frying pan and add the chicken pieces. Brown on all sides, then transfer to a casserole.

Add the onion, carrot and celery to the fat remaining in the pan and fry until the onion is softened. Sprinkle over the remaining flour and cook, stirring, for 3 minutes. Gradually stir in the stock and bring to the boil. Simmer, stirring, until thickened, then pour over the chicken.

Cover and cook in a preheated moderate oven, 180°C (350°F), for about 1 hour or until the chicken is tender.

Transfer the chicken pieces to a warmed serving dish and keep hot. Stir the cream into the sauce in the casserole and adjust the seasoning. Pour over the chicken.
Serves 4

Citrus Chicken

4 chicken quarters, skinned
salt and pepper
ground cinnamon
2 large lemons or limes
2 large oranges
30 g (1 oz) butter
parsley sprigs to garnish

Rub the chicken quarters with salt and pepper and a little cinnamon. Place in a greased casserole.

Squeeze the juice from one of the lemons or limes and pour over the chicken. Grate the rind from one of the oranges. Peel the remaining lemon or lime and both oranges and chop the flesh. Mix the flesh with the grated orange rind and pour over the chicken. Dot with the butter.

Cover tightly and cook in a pre-heated moderately hot oven, 190°C (375°F), for 1 hour or until tender. Garnish with parsley.
Serves 4

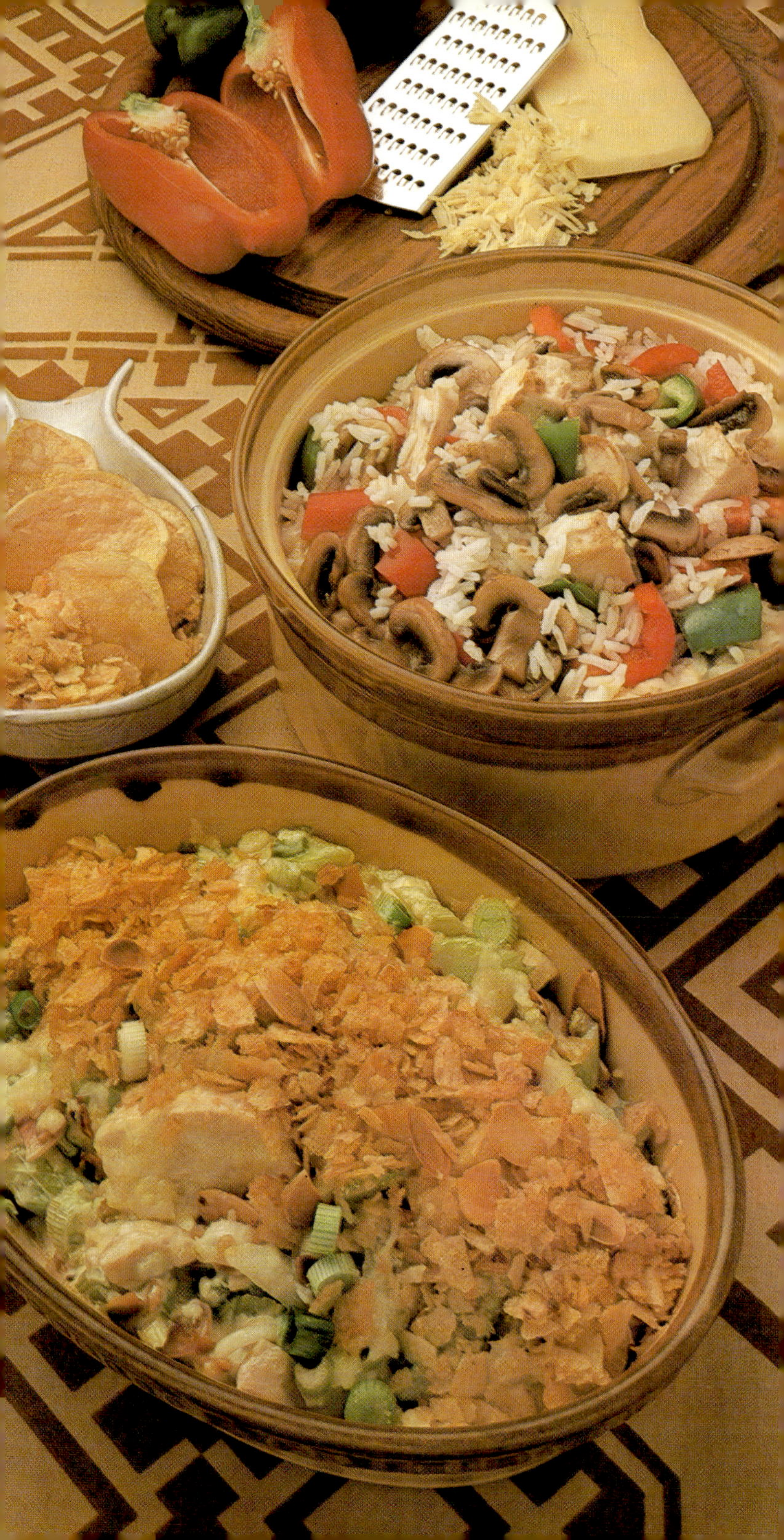

Chicken Pilaf

60 g (2 oz) butter
¼ cup plain flour
1 x 375 ml can evaporated milk
1¼ cups chicken stock
500 g (1 lb) cooked chicken meat, diced
8 cups cooked long-grain rice
125 g (4 oz) mushrooms, sliced
1 small green pepper, cored, seeded and diced
1 small red pepper, cored, seeded and diced
salt and pepper

Melt the butter in a saucepan. Add the flour and cook, stirring, for 2 minutes. Gradually stir in the evaporated milk and stock and bring to the boil. Simmer, stirring, until thickened.

Remove the sauce from the heat and fold in the chicken, rice, mushrooms, peppers and salt and pepper to taste. Turn into a greased casserole. Cover and cook in a preheated moderate oven, 180°C (350°F), for 45 minutes.

Serves 6 to 8

Crispy Chicken

500 g (1 lb) cooked chicken meat, chopped
4 celery sticks, chopped
⅔ cup mayonnaise
2 tablespoons lemon juice
4 spring onions, finely chopped
¼ cup slivered almonds, toasted
½ cup grated mature Cheddar cheese
salt and pepper
60 g (2 oz) potato crisps, crushed

Mix together the chicken, celery, mayonnaise, lemon juice, spring onions, almonds, cheese and salt and pepper to taste. Turn into a casserole. Sprinkle the crisps over the top and cook in a preheated moderately hot oven, 200°C (400°F), for 25 to 30 minutes or until piping hot.

Serves 4

Chicken with Sour Cream and Mushrooms

60 g (2 oz) butter
125 g (4 oz) mushrooms, sliced
¼ cup plain flour
⅔ cup dry white wine
1¼ cups milk (or mixed milk and cream)
⅔ cup sour cream
grated nutmeg
salt and pepper
8 half chicken breasts, skinned
chopped parsley to garnish

Melt the butter in a saucepan, add the mushrooms and sauté until just tender. Remove from the pan with a slotted spoon and set aside.

Add the flour to the fat remaining in the pan and cook, stirring, for 1 minute. Gradually stir in the wine and milk (or milk and cream) and bring to the boil. Simmer, stirring, until thickened. Add the mushrooms to the sauce, with the sour cream, and season to taste with nutmeg, salt and pepper.

Arrange the chicken breasts in a casserole. Pour over the sauce. Cover and cook in a preheated moderate oven, 180°C (350°F), for 45 minutes or until the chicken is tender. Serve garnished with the remaining mushrooms and parsley.
Serves 4 to 6

Spicy Chicken with Fruit

3 tablespoons plain flour
salt and pepper
4 chicken quarters
60 g (2 oz) butter
1 onion, thinly sliced
1 tablespoon chilli seasoning (or more to taste)
1 x 215 g can tomatoes
⅔ cup chicken stock
2 fresh peaches, peeled, stoned and sliced (or use canned peach slices)
3 bananas, thinly sliced

Season the flour and use to coat the chicken quarters. Melt the butter in a frying pan and brown the chicken quarters on all sides, then transfer to a casserole.

Add the onion to the pan and fry until softened. Stir in the chilli seasoning, tomatoes with their juice, and stock. Bring to the boil. Season with salt and pepper to taste and stir in the peaches and bananas. Pour this mixture over the chicken quarters.

Cover and cook in a preheated moderate oven, 180°C (350°F), for 1¼ to 1½ hours or until the chicken is tender.
Serves 4

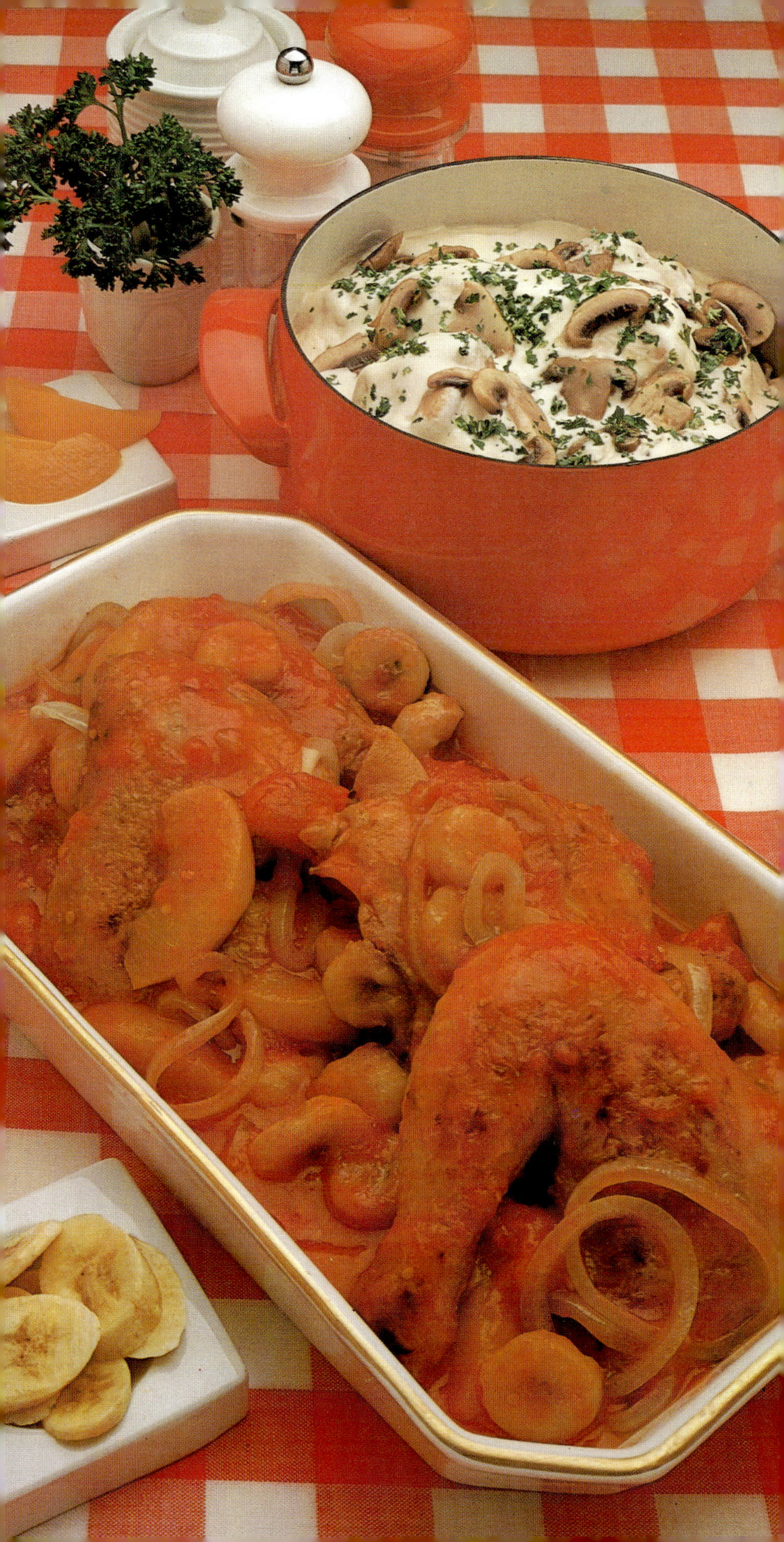

VEGETABLES

Tomatoes with Parmesan and Cream

8 large tomatoes, skinned and sliced
3 tablespoons medium sherry
½ teaspoon sugar
salt and pepper
¼ cup grated Parmesan cheese
⅔ cup cream
parsley sprigs to garnish

Arrange the tomato slices in a greased small casserole. Sprinkle with the sherry, sugar and salt and pepper to taste, then the Parmesan. Pour the cream over the top.

Cook in a preheated moderately hot oven, 200°C (400°F), for about 20 minutes. Serve garnished with parsley sprigs.

Serves 4

Eggplant and bacon casserole; Tomatoes with Parmesan and cream; Broccoli lorraine (page 72).

Eggplant and Bacon Casserole

750 g (1½ lb) eggplant, cut into 1 cm (½ inch) slices
salt and pepper
5 tablespoons oil (approximately)
250 g (8 oz) streaky bacon rashers, derinded and diced
1 large onion, chopped
1 clove garlic, crushed
1 medium green pepper, cored, seeded and diced
250 g (8 oz) mushrooms, sliced
1 x 400 g can tomatoes
½ teaspoon dried thyme
1 teaspoon sugar
125 g (4 oz) shredded Mozzarella or Gruyère cheese

Sprinkle the eggplant slices with salt and leave to drain for 30 minutes. Rinse and pat dry.

Brush a baking sheet with a little of the oil and arrange the eggplant slices on top in a single layer. Brush with the remaining oil. Cook in a preheated hot oven, 230°C (450°F), for 35 minutes.

Meanwhile, fry the bacon in a frying pan until crisp, then remove.

Add the onion, garlic and green pepper to the pan and fry until the onion is softened. Stir in the mushrooms, tomatoes, with their juice, thyme, salt and pepper to taste and the sugar. Simmer until the mixture is quite thick, stirring occasionally.

Layer the eggplant slices, bacon and tomato sauce in a shallow casserole. Top with the cheese.

Reduce the oven temperature to moderate, 180°C (350°F), and cook for 20 minutes or until beginning to brown.

Serves 4 to 6

Broccoli Lorraine

750 g (1½ lb) broccoli, cut into 5 cm (2 inch) pieces
15 g (½ oz) butter
4 bacon rashers, derinded and diced
1 onion, thinly sliced
1¼ cups milk
⅔ cup cream
4 eggs, beaten
¼ cup grated Gruyère cheese
salt and pepper

Arrange the broccoli in a greased casserole. Melt the butter in a frying pan, add the bacon and fry until crisp. Remove the bacon with a slotted spoon and sprinkle on top of the broccoli.

Fry the onion in the fat remaining in the pan until golden, then remove with a slotted spoon and scatter over the broccoli.

Mix together the milk, cream, eggs, cheese and salt and pepper to taste, then pour into the casserole.

Place the casserole in a roasting pan, containing about 2.5 cm (1 inch) of boiling water. Cook in a preheated moderate oven, 180°C (350°F), for 30 minutes or until just set.

Serves 4 to 6

Illustrated on page 71.

Swede and Apple Casserole

750 g (1½ lb) swede, cubed
salt and pepper
1 large cooking apple, peeled, cored and sliced
⅓ cup brown sugar
30 g (1 oz) butter
3 to 4 tablespoons medium sherry (optional)

Cook the swede in boiling salted water for 20 to 30 minutes or until just tender. Drain well.

Put half the swede in a greased casserole and cover with half the apple slices. Sprinkle over half the brown sugar and salt and pepper to taste. Dot with half the butter. Repeat the layers. Sprinkle over the sherry, if using.

Cover and cook in a preheated moderate oven, 180°C (350°F), for 30 minutes.

Serves 4

Pineapple Parsnips

1 kg (2 lb) parsnips, quartered lengthways
⅔ cup unsweetened pineapple juice
1 teaspoon sugar
salt and pepper
45 g (1½ oz) butter

Cut the cores from the parsnips, then place in a greased baking dish. Mix together the pineapple juice, sugar and salt and pepper to taste and pour over the parsnips. Dot with the butter. Cover and cook in a preheated moderate oven, 180°C (350°F), for 1 hour or until the parsnips are tender.
Serves 4 to 6

Green Peppers and Beans

500 g (1 lb) green beans (stringed if necessary)
2 green peppers, cored, seeded and chopped
2 onions, finely chopped
salt and pepper
dried thyme
45 g (1½ oz) butter

If the beans are large, cut in half. Make alternate layers of the vegetables in a greased casserole, beginning and ending with beans. Sprinkle each layer with salt and pepper and a little thyme and dot with butter.

Cover tightly and cook in a preheated moderate oven, 180°C (350°F), for 1 hour or until the vegetables are very tender.
Serves 4

Red Cabbage with Apple

1 kg (2 lb) red cabbage, cored and shredded
45 g (1½ oz) butter
1 onion, sliced
2 medium cooking apples, peeled, cored and sliced
3 tablespoons water
3 tablespoons wine vinegar
4 teaspoons sugar
salt and pepper
1 tablespoon plain flour
chopped parsley to garnish

Blanch the cabbage in boiling water for 1 minute, then drain well. Melt 30 g (1 oz) of the butter in a flameproof casserole. Add the onion and fry until softened. Add the apples and fry for a further 5 minutes. Remove from the casserole with a slotted spoon.

Make alternate layers of the cabbage and apple mixture in the casserole, beginning and ending with cabbage. Sprinkle each layer with water, vinegar, sugar, salt and pepper. Cover tightly and cook in a preheated moderate oven, 160°C (325°F), for 2 hours, stirring occasionally and adding more water if necessary.

Blend the remaining butter with the flour to make a paste. Mix with a little of the liquid from the casserole, then stir this into the casserole. Cook gently on top of the stove until thickened. Garnish with parsley.
Serves 4

Broad Beans with Walnuts

1 kg (2 lb) fresh broad beans, shelled
salt and pepper
30 g (1 oz) butter
1 small onion, finely chopped
⅔ cup chicken stock
2 cups grated Cheddar cheese
1½ teaspoons French mustard
1 teaspoon Worcestershire sauce
1 cup chopped walnuts

Cook the beans in boiling salted water for 15 to 20 minutes or until just tender. Drain well.

Melt the butter in a clean saucepan. Add the onion and fry until softened. Stir in the stock and bring to the boil. Add the cheese, stir until melted, then mix in the mustard, Worcestershire sauce and salt and pepper to taste. Fold in the walnuts and beans.

Turn into a greased casserole. Cook in a preheated moderate oven, 180°C (359°F), for 30 minutes.
Serves 4

Stuffed Cabbage

1 medium cabbage
2 tablespoons olive oil
4 bacon rashers, derinded and chopped
1 onion, chopped
1 clove garlic, crushed
1 egg, beaten
2 tablespoons grated Parmesan cheese
3 tablespoons chopped parsley
salt and pepper
1 cup chicken stock

Cook the whole cabbage in boiling water for 15 minutes. Drain and cool under cold running water. Cut out the core, then remove the inner cabbage leaves, leaving the outside leaves intact. Chop the inner leaves.

Heat the oil in a frying pan, add the chopped cabbage leaves, bacon, onion and garlic and fry until the onion is softened. Remove from the heat. Mix together the egg, cheese, parsley and salt and pepper to taste and stir into the cabbage mixture.

Place the cabbage 'shell' of large outside leaves in a casserole lined with foil and fill the shell with the fried mixture. Pour over the stock. Cover and cook in a preheated moderately hot oven, 190°C (375°F), for 1 hour. Uncover the casserole and cook for a further 30 minutes. To serve, lift the cabbage out, then remove the foil.
Serves 6 to 8

Scalloped Potatoes

8 medium potatoes, thinly sliced
1 medium onion, thinly sliced
5 tablespoons plain flour
salt and pepper
2½ cups milk
4 tablespoons dry breadcrumbs
15 g (½ oz) butter, melted

Make a layer of about one third of the potato slices in a greased casserole. Sprinkle with one third of the onion and flour and season with salt and pepper to taste. Repeat these layers twice, then pour over the milk.

Mix the breadcrumbs with the butter and sprinkle over the top. Cover and cook in a preheated moderate oven, 180°C (350°F), for 1¼ hours.

Remove the lid and continue cooking for 15 minutes or until the top is crisp and golden brown.
Serves 6

Zucchini Casserole

1 kg (2 lb) zucchini
salt and pepper
1 teaspoon dried oregano
1 cup grated mature Cheddar cheese
½ cup chopped, blanched almonds
30 g (1 oz) butter, melted

Steam the zucchini until just tender. Cut into 1 cm (½ inch) slices and layer a quarter of these in a greased casserole. Sprinkle with salt and pepper and a quarter of the oregano. Cover with a quarter of the cheese. Continue making layers in this way, ending with cheese.

Mix together the nuts and butter and scatter over the top. Cook in a preheated moderate oven, 180°C (350°F), for 20 minutes.

Serves 4 to 6

Sweetcorn Pudding

375 g (12 oz) frozen or canned sweetcorn
2 cups milk
3 eggs, beaten
1 small onion, grated
1 teaspoon sugar
15 g (½ oz) butter, melted
salt and pepper
parsley sprigs to garnish

If using frozen sweetcorn, allow it to thaw; drain canned sweetcorn. Mix together all the ingredients with salt and pepper to taste. Turn into a greased casserole. Place in a baking tin containing 2.5 cm (1 inch) water.

Cook in a preheated moderate oven, 180°C (350°F), for about 45 minutes or until a knife inserted into the centre comes out clean. Garnish with parsley.

Serves 4 to 6

Spinach and Bacon Bake

750 g (1½ lb) spinach
4 streaky bacon rashers, derinded and diced
125 g (4 oz) mushrooms, sliced
salt and pepper
½ teaspoon dried thyme
1¼ cups sour cream
¼ cup grated mature Cheddar cheese
¼ cup grated Parmesan cheese

Cook the spinach, with just the water clinging to the leaves after washing, until tender. Drain well, pressing out all the excess moisture, then chop. Spread the chopped spinach over the bottom of a greased casserole.

Fry the bacon in a dry frying pan until crisp. Drain on kitchen paper and sprinkle over the spinach. Cover with the mushrooms, then season with salt and pepper to taste and sprinkle with the thyme. Cook in a preheated moderate oven, 160°C (325°F), for 15 minutes.

Pour over the cream. Mix together the Parmesan and Cheddar cheese and scatter over the top. Return to the oven and cook for a further 10 minutes or until the cheese is melted.
Serves 4 to 6

PULSES, RICE, PASTA & CHEESE

Fettucine Casserole

250 g (8 oz) green noodles (fettucine verde)
salt and pepper
2 tablespoons olive oil
1 onion, chopped
1 clove garlic, crushed (optional)
125 g (4 oz) mushrooms, sliced
250 g (8 oz) Mortadella sausage, finely chopped
250 g (8 oz) Ricotta or cottage cheese
1 egg
125 g (4 oz) shredded Mozzarella or Gruyère cheese

Cook the noodles in boiling salted water until just tender.

Meanwhile, heat the oil in a frying pan, add the onion and garlic (if using) and fry until softened. Add the mushrooms and fry for a further 3 minutes, then stir in the sausage. Remove from the heat.

Drain the noodles and fold into the sausage mixture. Beat the Ricotta cheese and egg together and stir into the sausage mixture with salt and pepper to taste. Turn into a casserole and top with the Mozzarella cheese. Bake in a preheated moderate oven, 160°C (325°F), for 35 minutes.

Serves 4

Macaroni cheese with sour cream; Fettucine casserole; Lasagne (page 82).

Macaroni Cheese with Sour Cream

250 g (8 oz) macaroni
salt and pepper
30 g (1 oz) butter, melted
1 cup grated mature Cheddar cheese
⅔ cup sour cream
4 tablespoons milk
1 egg, beaten
pinch of paprika

Cook the macaroni in boiling salted water until tender. Drain well, then mix with the butter and salt and pepper to taste. Make alternate layers of macaroni and cheese in a casserole, reserving about 2 tablespoons of the cheese for the topping.

Mix together the sour cream, milk, egg, paprika and salt and pepper to taste. Pour over the macaroni and scatter the remaining cheese on top. Cook in a preheated moderately hot oven, 200°C (400°F), for about 20 minutes or until the top is golden brown.
Serves 4

Lasagne

2 tablespoons olive oil
2 onions, chopped
1 clove garlic, crushed
750 g (1½ lb) minced beef
2 x 400 g cans tomatoes
4 tablespoons tomato paste
⅔ cup water
1½ teaspoons sugar
2 teaspoons dried mixed herbs
1 bay leaf
salt and pepper
250 g (8 oz) mushrooms, sliced
500 g (1 lb) lasagne
500 g (1 lb) Ricotta or cottage cheese
500 g (1 lb) sliced Mozzarella or Gruyère cheese
2 cups grated Parmesan cheese

Heat the oil in a frying pan, add the onions and garlic and fry until softened. Add the beef and fry until well browned, then stir in the tomatoes with their juice, tomato paste, water, sugar, herbs and salt and pepper to taste. Bring to the boil and simmer gently for 1¼ hours. Stir in the mushrooms and simmer for 20 minutes. Discard the bay leaf.

Just before the sauce is ready, cook the lasagne, in batches, in boiling salted water. (A little oil added to the water will prevent the sheets of pasta sticking together.) Drain well.

Spoon a little of the sauce over the bottom of a shallow baking dish. Cover with a layer of lasagne, then a layer each of the Ricotta, Mozzarella and Parmesan cheeses. Continue making layers in this way, ending with lasagne sprinkled with Parmesan. Cook in a preheated moderate oven, 180°C (350°F), for 1 hour.

Serves 8 to 10

Illustrated on page 81.

Noodles Paprika

185 g (6 oz) noodles
salt and pepper
15 g (½ oz) butter
1 medium onion, finely chopped
1 clove garlic, crushed
2 teaspoons paprika
250 g (8 oz) cottage cheese
1¼ cups sour cream
few drops of Tabasco sauce
1 teaspoon caraway seeds (optional)
paprika to garnish

Cook the noodles in boiling salted water until just tender. Drain well. Melt the butter in a frying pan, add the onion and garlic and fry until softened. Stir in the paprika. Cook, stirring, for 1 minute.

Remove from the heat and stir in the cottage cheese, sour cream, Tabasco and salt and pepper to taste. Add the caraway seeds (if using). Fold in the noodles.

Turn into a greased casserole and cook in a preheated moderate oven, 180°C (350°F), for 30 minutes. Sprinkle with paprika to garnish.

Serves 4 to 6

Cheese Charlotte

90 g (3 oz) butter
12 x 1 cm (½ inch) thick slices white bread, crusts removed
1 cup grated mature Cheddar cheese
1½ cups milk
2 eggs, beaten
salt and pepper
pinch of dry mustard
2 tablespoons chopped fresh chives

Butter all the bread slices. Cut 4 or 5 slices into 2.5 cm (1 inch) wide fingers and use to line a deep, straight-sided casserole, buttered side against the casserole. Cut the remaining slices into cubes.

Make alternate layers of bread cubes and grated cheese in the casserole. Mix together the milk, eggs, salt and pepper to taste, mustard and chives and pour into the casserole.

Cook in a preheated moderate oven, 180°C (350°F), for 30 minutes.
Serves 4

Italian Baked Beans

2½ cups dried white haricot beans, soaked overnight
125 g (4 oz) Mortadella sausage, chopped
2 cloves garlic, crushed
2 teaspoons dried oregano
salt and pepper
4 tablespoons tomato paste
2½ cups water (approximately)

Drain the beans and mix with the sausage, garlic, oregano and salt and pepper to taste. Mix the tomato paste with the water.

Put the bean mixture in a casserole and stir in enough water to just cover the beans.

Cover and cook in a preheated cool oven, 140°C (275°F), for 3 to 3½ hours or until the beans are tender. If necessary, add a little more water to the casserole during cooking.
Serves 6

Boston Baked Beans

2½ cups dried haricot beans, soaked overnight
8 cups water
salt and pepper
½ cup brown sugar
1 teaspoon dry mustard
5 tablespoons treacle
125 g (4 oz) salt pork, chopped
1 medium onion, chopped

Drain the beans and put in a saucepan with the water and ½ teaspoon salt. Bring to the boil, then cover and simmer for about 1 hour or until the beans are tender. Drain, reserving the liquid.

Mix together the sugar, mustard, treacle, 2½ cups of the reserved cooking liquid and salt and pepper to taste. Put the beans, salt pork and onion in a casserole and stir in the treacle mixture.

Cover and cook in a preheated cool oven, 150°C (300°F), for 4 hours, stirring occasionally and adding more of the reserved cooking liquid if necessary, during cooking.
Serves 6 to 8

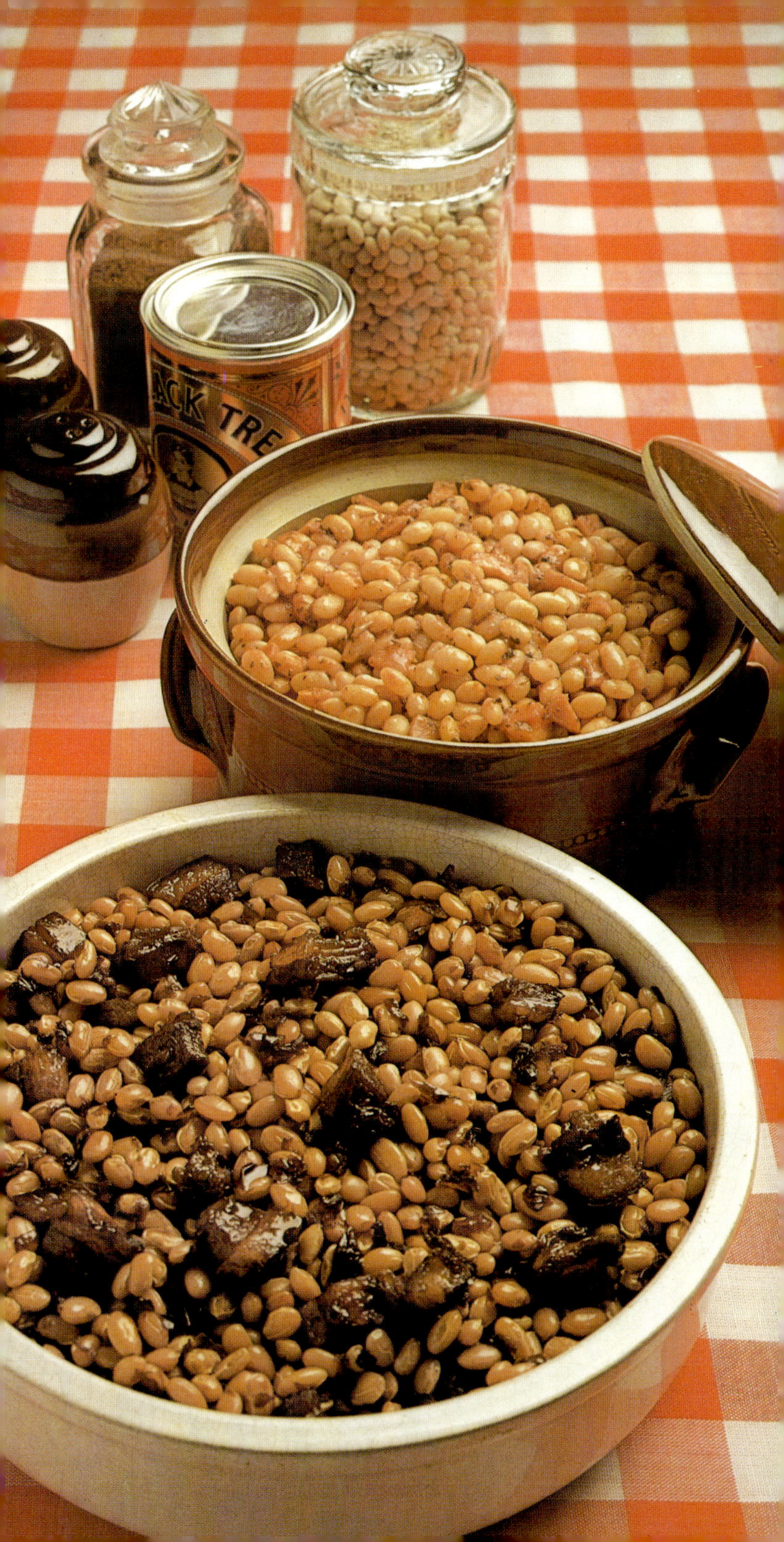

Curried Rice

1½ cups long-grain rice
4 cups water
1 onion, finely chopped
2 celery sticks, coarsely chopped
250 g (8 oz) tomatoes, skinned and chopped
1½ teaspoons salt
1½ teaspoons mild curry powder (or more to taste)
60 g (2 oz) butter, melted

Put the rice in a casserole and pour over the water. Leave to soak for 45 minutes.

Stir the remaining ingredients into the rice. Cook in a preheated moderate oven, 180°C (350°F), for 1½ hours or until the rice is tender and all the liquid has been absorbed.
Serves 6

Layered Lentil Casserole

2½ cups lentils, soaked overnight
1 bay leaf
6 slices cooked ham or gammon, cut into strips
1 teaspoon dried thyme
salt and pepper
375 g (12 oz) cooked chicken meat, cut into strips
1¼ cups chicken stock (approximately)
¼ cup grated Parmesan cheese
¼ cup dry breadcrumbs

Drain the lentils and put into a saucepan with the bay leaf. Add fresh water to cover and bring to the boil. Simmer gently for about 1 hour or until tender. Drain the lentils, discarding the bay leaf.

Put about one third of the lentils in a greased casserole. Cover with the ham and sprinkle with half the thyme and salt and pepper to taste. Cover with another third of the lentils, then add the chicken. Sprinkle with the rest of the thyme and salt and pepper to taste.

Top with the remaining lentils and pour in the stock. Cover and cook in a preheated moderate oven, 180°C (350°F), for 30 minutes.

Mix together the cheese and breadcrumbs and sprinkle over the top. Cook, uncovered, for 15 minutes or until the topping is golden brown.
Serves 4 to 6

Haricot Bean and Sweetcorn Casserole

1¼ cups dried haricot beans, soaked overnight
1 x 400 g can sweetcorn, drained
1 x 400 g can tomatoes, drained
salt and pepper
1 tablespoon brown sugar
1 tablespoon grated onion
¼ cup browned breadcrumbs

Drain the beans and place in a saucepan. Cover with fresh water, bring to the boil and simmer for 45 minutes or until tender.

Drain the beans and mix with the sweetcorn, tomatoes, salt and pepper to taste, sugar and onion. Turn into a greased casserole and sprinkle the breadcrumbs over the top. Cook in a preheated moderate oven, 180°C (350°F), for 45 minutes.

Serves 4

Fruit and Nut Pilaf

½ cup sultanas
185 g (6 oz) dried fruit (apricots, apples, pears, etc.)
1 tablespoon sweet sherry
90 g (3 oz) butter
1 onion, finely chopped
6 cups cooked long-grain rice
½ teaspoon ground allspice
salt and pepper
½ cup flaked almonds

Put the sultanas and dried fruit in a bowl, sprinkle with the sherry and cover with water. Leave to soak for 4 hours. Drain and chop the apricots, apples or pears.

Melt the butter in a frying pan, add the onion and fry until softened. Stir in the rice and allspice, then add salt and pepper to taste and mix well.

Fold in the fruit and almonds, then turn the mixture into a greased casserole. Bake in a preheated moderately hot oven, 190°C (375°F), for 30 minutes.

Serves 6

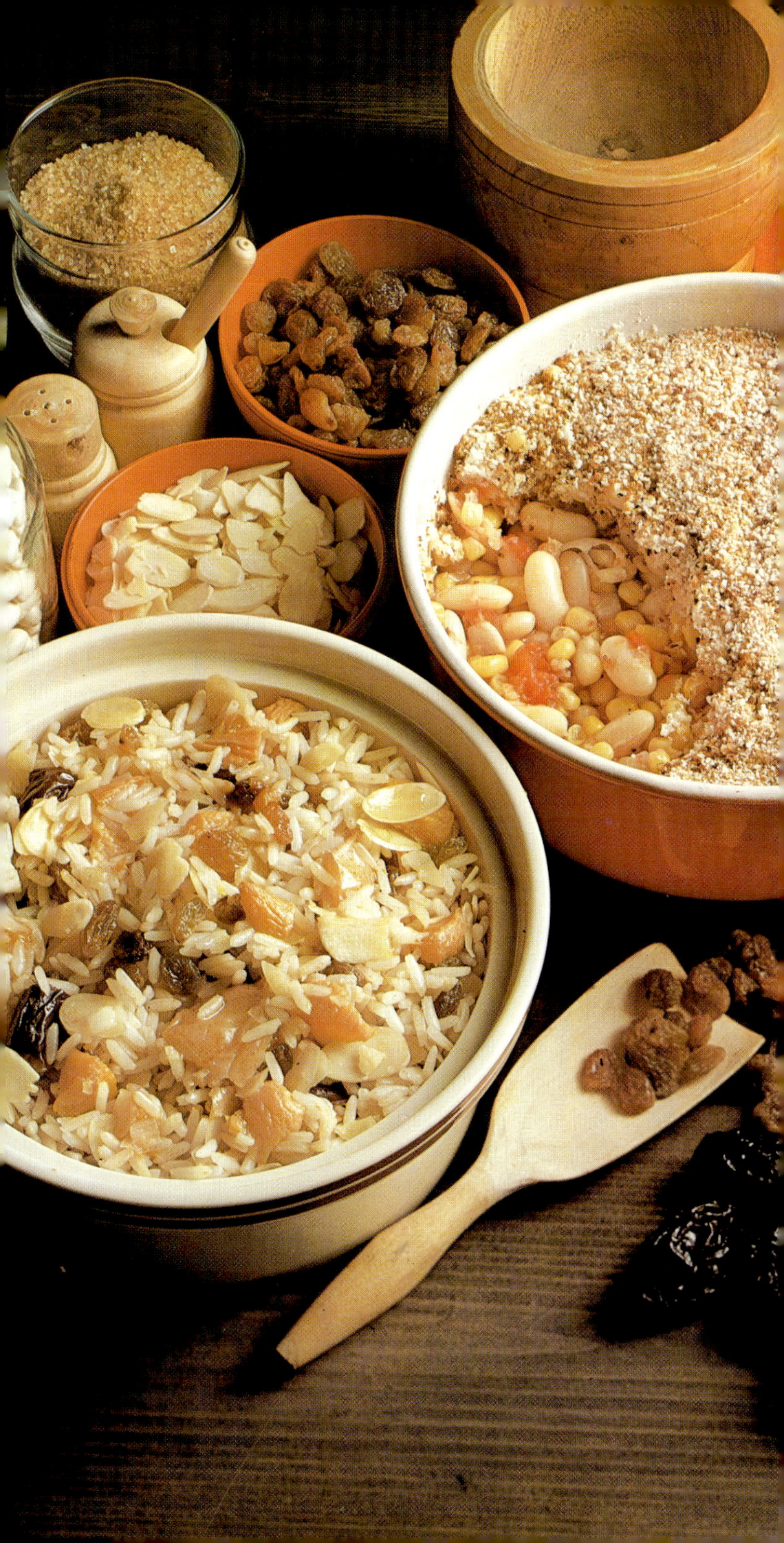

Rice with Parsley and Cheese

4 cups cooked
  long-grain rice
6 spring onions,
  finely chopped
40 g (1½ oz)
  chopped parsley
3 eggs, beaten
4 tablespoons milk
1 cup grated Cheddar
  cheese
salt and pepper

Mix together the rice, spring onions and parsley. Combine the remaining ingredients with salt and pepper to taste and add to the rice mixture. Blend well, then turn into a greased casserole. Cook in a preheated moderate oven, 180°C (350°F), for 30 minutes or until just set.
Serves 4

Pearl Barley Casserole

60 g (2 oz) butter
2 medium leeks,
  thinly sliced
1 green pepper,
  cored, seeded and
  chopped
1¼ cups pearl barley
60 g (2 oz) cooked
  ham, diced
  (optional)
1 x 300 g can
  sweetcorn, drained
1¼ cups chicken
  stock
salt and pepper

Melt the butter in a flameproof casserole. Add the leeks and green pepper and fry until softened. Stir in the remaining ingredients with salt and pepper to taste.
  Cover and cook in a preheated moderate oven, 160°C (325°F), for 40 minutes or until the barley is tender and all the liquid absorbed.
Serves 4

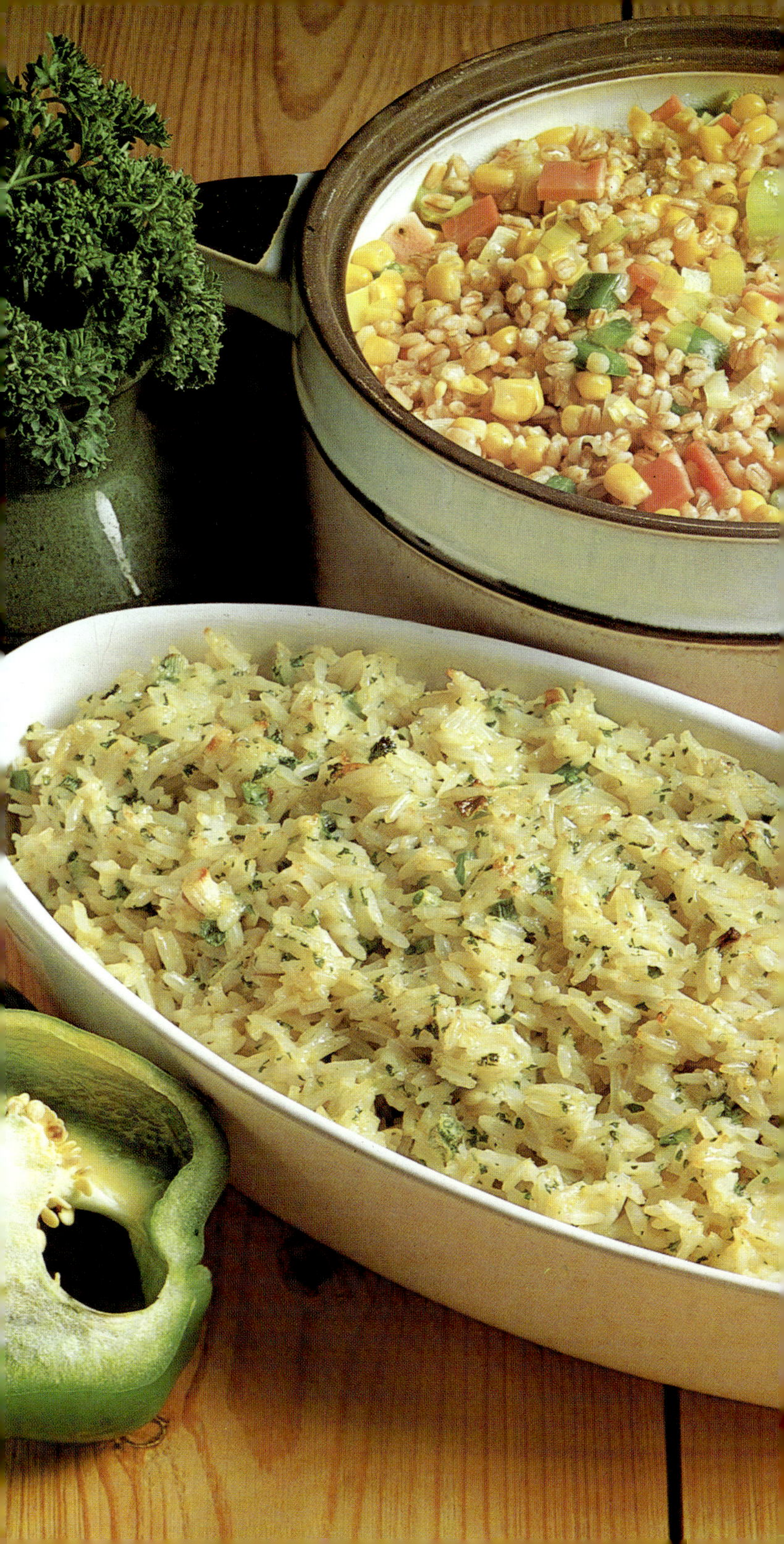

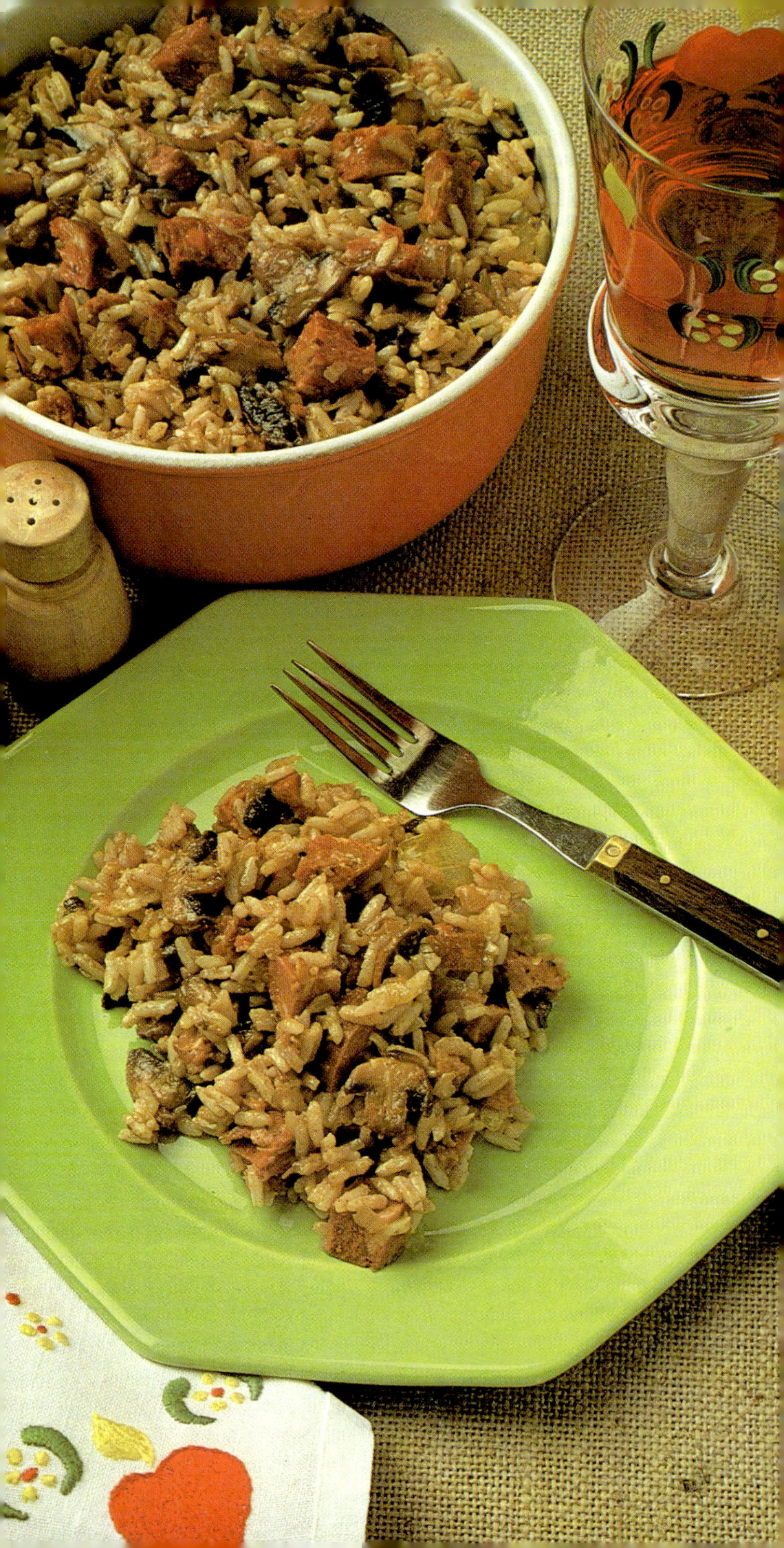

Spanish Rice Casserole

5 tablespoons olive oil
1 onion, finely chopped
1 clove garlic, crushed
1¼ cups long-grain rice
1 tablespoon chilli powder (or to taste)
salt and pepper
125 g (4 oz) chorizo or garlic sausage, diced
125 g (4 oz) small button mushrooms
2 cups boiling stock (approximately)

Heat the oil in a flameproof casserole, add the onion and garlic and fry until softened. Stir in the rice, chilli powder and salt and pepper to taste. Cook, stirring, until the rice is golden. Add the chorizo or garlic sausage and mushrooms and mix well. Add enough stock to come about 2.5 cm (1 inch) above the level of the rice; stir thoroughly.

Cover tightly and cook in a preheated moderate oven, 180°C (350°F), for 30 minutes or until the rice is tender and the liquid absorbed.

Serves 4

INDEX

Arroz con pollo 61

Bacon:
  Eggplant and bacon casserole 71
  Liver and bacon hotpot 41
  Spinach and bacon bake 79
Barbecued spare rib casserole 48
Barley casserole, Pearl 90
Beans:
  Boston baked beans 84
  Broad beans with walnuts 75
  Green peppers and beans 74
  Haricot bean and sweetcorn casserole 88
  Haricot of lamb 45
  Italian baked beans 84
  Sausage and bean casserole 50
Beef 20-29
Beef and spinach bake 23
Beef carbonnade 29
Beef casserole with horseradish 28
Beef olives 22
Beef stroganoff casserole 28
Boston baked beans 84
Bream with grapefruit and mushrooms 13
Broad beans with walnuts 75
Broccoli Lorraine 72

Cabbage, Stuffed 76
Cabbage with apple, Red 75
Cheese charlotte 83
Chicken 59-69
Chicken pilaf 67
Chicken with sour cream and mushrooms 68
Chilli-pasta casserole 26
Chilli pork 49
Cidered sausages 51
Citrus chicken 65
Cod and celery bake, Salt 15
Cod casserole, Herby 11
Coq au vin 60
Crab and spaghetti bake 19
Crispy chicken 67
Curried chicken casserole 61
Curried rice 86

Daube de boeuf 25
Duckling and orange casserole 55

Eggplant:
  Eggplant and bacon casserole 71
  Moussaka 40

Fettucine casserole 80
Fish 6-19
Fish au gratin, Smoked 14
Fish boulangère 13
Fish mornay 10
Fish with horseradish cream 15
Fruit and nut pilaf 88

Game and poultry 54-69
Gemfish in cider 16
Gingered beef 27
Golden-top casserole 31
Goulash, Veal 32
Grapefruit chicken 64
Greek prawn casserole 9
Green peppers and beans 74

Ham and egg pie 51
Hare:
  Hunter's casserole 58
Haricot bean and sweetcorn casserole 88
Haricot of lamb 45
Herby fish casserole 11
Hunter's casserole 58

Italian baked beans 84
Italian beef casserole 21
Italian pot roast 20

Japanese chicken casserole 59

Kidney ragoût 37

Lamb 36-45
Lamb chops with apples 42
Lamb, Pork and potato casserole 43
Lamb ratatouille 38
Lamb stew 36
Lamb with mushrooms and tomatoes 44
Lasagne 82

Lemon beef stew 24
Lentil casserole, Layered 87
Liver and bacon hotpot 41

Macaroni cheese with sour cream 81
Meatball casserole 34
Mediterranean fish steaks 8
Mexican chilli-pasta casserole 26
Moussaka 40

Noodles:
  Fettucine casserole 80
  Noodles paprika 82
  Tuna noodle casserole 16

Orange lamb casserole 38
Oxtail casserole 25

Parsnips, Pineapple 73
Pearl barley casserole 90
Pheasant, Casseroled 54
Pineapple parsnips 73
Plummy pork chops 46
Pork 43, 46-53. *See also* Bacon
Pork and apple casserole 52
Pork and green beans 47
Pork casseroled with fruit 53
Pork in mushroom sauce 48
Pot roast, Italian 20
Potatoes, Scalloped 77
Poultry and game 54-69
Prawn casserole, Greek 9
Prawns in herb butter 7

Rabbit in cranberry sauce 56
Rabbit with mustard sauce 57
Red cabbage with apple 75
Rice:
  Arroz con pollo 61
  Chicken pilaf 67
  Curried rice 86

Fruit and nut pilaf 88
Rice with parsley and cheese 90
Spanish rice casserole 93
Roman veal casserole 35

Salt cod and celery bake 15
Sausage and bean casserole 50
Sausages, Cidered 51
Scalloped potatoes 77
Shellfish casserole 8
Smoked fish au gratin 14
Smothered chicken 64
Spanish rice casserole 93
Spicy chicken with fruit 68
Spinach:
  Beef and spinach bake 23
  Spinach and bacon bake 79
Spring chicken casserole 62
Swede and apple casserole 72
Sweetbreads, Braised 30
Sweetcorn:
  Haricot bean and sweetcorn casserole 88
  Sweetcorn pudding 78

Tomatoes with Parmesan and cream 70
Tuna noodle casserole 16
Turkey bake 56

Veal 30-35
Veal goulash 32
Veal Parmesan 32
Veal with orange 33
Vegetables 23, 70-79

Welsh chicken casserole 63
Whole fish with tomato sauce 6

Zucchini casserole 78

Acknowledgments

Recipes devised by Norma MacMillan
Photography by Frederick Mancini
Food prepared by Heather Lambert